VIOLIN
MASTERY

EUGÈNE YSAYE

Cordial souvenir à Mr Fr. H. Martens
Avec toute ma gratitude pour les
Services éminents que ses beaux articles
rendent à notre art.
New York Sept. 1918

VIOLIN MASTERY

INTERVIEWS WITH
HEIFETZ, AUER, KREISLER
AND OTHERS

FREDERICK H. MARTENS

DOVER PUBLICATIONS, INC.
Mineola, New York

Bibliographical Note

This Dover edition, first published in 2006, is an unabridged republication of the work originally published by Frederick A. Stokes Co., New York, in 1919.

International Standard Book Number: 0-486-45041-4

Manufactured in the United States by Courier Corporation
45041404
www.doverpublications.com

Contents

Illustrations

FOREWORD

The appreciation accorded Miss Harriette Brower's admirable books on PIANO MASTERY has prompted the present volume of intimate *Talks with Master Violinists and Teachers*, in which a number of famous artists and instructors discuss æsthetic and technical phases of the art of violin playing in detail, their concept of what Violin Mastery means, and how it may be acquired. Only limitation of space has prevented the inclusion of numerous other deserving artists and teachers, yet practically all of the greatest masters of the violin now in this country are represented. That the lessons of their artistry and experience will be of direct benefit and value to every violin student and every lover of violin music may be accepted as a foregone conclusion.

FREDERICK H. MARTENS.

171 Orient Way,
Rutherford, N.J.

FOREWORD

EUGÈNE YSAYE

THE TOOLS OF VIOLIN MASTERY

W ho is there among contemporary masters of the violin whose name stands for more at the present time than that of the great Belgian artist, his "extraordinary temperamental power as an interpreter" enhanced by a hundred and one special gifts of tone and technique, gifts often alluded to by his admiring colleagues? For Ysaye is the greatest exponent of that wonderful Belgian school of violin playing which is rooted in his teachers Vieuxtemps and Wieniawski, and which as Ysaye himself says, "during a period covering seventy years reigned supreme at the *Conservatoire* in Paris in the persons of Massart, Remi, Marsick, and others of its great interpreters."

What most impresses one who meets Ysaye and talks with him for the first time is the mental breadth and vision of the man; his kindness and amiability; his utter lack of small vanity. When the writer first called on him in New York with a note of introduction from his friend and admirer Adolfo Betti, and later at Scarsdale where, in company with his friend Thibaud, he was dividing his time between music and tennis, Ysaye made him entirely at home, and willingly talked of his art and its ideals. In reply to some questions anent his own study years, he said:

"Strange to say, my father was my very first teacher—it is not often the case. I studied with him until I went to the Liège Conservatory in 1867, where I won a second prize, sharing it with Ovide Musin, for playing Viotti's 22d Concerto. Then I had lessons from Wieniawski in Brussels and studied two years with Vieuxtemps in Paris. Vieuxtemps was a paralytic when I came to

1

him; yet a wonderful teacher, though he could no longer play. And I was already a concertizing artist when I met him. He was a very great man, the grandeur of whose tradition lives in the whole 'romantic school' of violin playing. Look at his seven concertos—of course they are written with an eye to effect, from the virtuoso's standpoint, yet how firmly and solidly they are built up! How interesting is their working-out: and the orchestral score is far more than a mere accompaniment. As regards virtuose effect only Paganini's music compares with his, and Paganini, of course, did not play it as it is now played. In wealth of technical development, in true musical expressiveness Vieuxtemps is a master. A proof is the fact that his works have endured forty to fifty years, a long life for compositions.

"Joachim, Léonard, Sivori, Wieniawski—all admired Vieuxtemps. In Paganini's and Locatelli's works the effect, comparatively speaking, lies in the mechanics; but Vieuxtemps is the great artist who made the instrument take the road of romanticism which Hugo, Balzac and Gauthier trod in literature. And before all the violin was made to charm, to move, and Vieuxtemps knew it. Like Rubinstein, he held that the artist must first of all have ideas, emotional power—his technique must be so perfected that he does not have to think of it! Incidentally, speaking of schools of violin playing, I find that there is a great tendency to confuse the Belgian and French. This should not be. They are distinct, though the latter has undoubtedly been formed and influenced by the former. Many of the great violin names, in fact,—Vieuxtemps, Léonard, Marsick, Remi, Parent, de Broux, Musin, Thomson,—are all Belgian."

YSAYE'S REPERTORY

Ysaye spoke of Vieuxtemps's repertory—only he did not call it that: he spoke of the Vieuxtemps compositions and of Vieuxtemps himself. "Vieuxtemps wrote in the grand style; his music is always rich and sonorous. If his violin is really to sound, the violinist must play Vieuxtemps, just as the 'cellist plays Servais. You know, in the Catholic Church, at Vespers, whenever God's name is spoken, we bow the head. And Wieniawski would always bow his head when he said: 'Vieuxtemps is the master of us all!'

"I have often played his *Fifth Concerto,* so warm, brilliant and replete with temperament, always full-sounding, rich in an almost unbounded strength. Of course, since Vieuxtemps wrote his concertos, a great variety of fine modern works has appeared, the appreciation of chamber-music has grown and developed, and with it that of the sonata. And the modern violin sonata is also a vehicle for violin virtuosity in the very best meaning of the word. The sonatas of César Franck, d'Indy, Théodore Dubois, Lekeu, Vierne, Ropartz, Lazarri—they are all highly expressive, yet at the same time virtuose. The violin parts develop a lovely song line, yet their technique is far from simple. Take Lekeu's splendid *Sonata in G major*; rugged and massive, making decided technical demands—it yet has a wonderful breadth of melody, a great expressive quality of song."

These works—those who have heard the Master play the beautiful Lazarri sonata this season will not soon forget it—are all dedicated to Ysaye. And this holds good, too, of the César Franck sonata. As Ysaye says: "Performances of these great sonatas call for *two* artists—for their piano parts are sometimes very elaborate. César Franck sent me his sonata on September 26, 1886, my wedding day—it was his wedding present! I cannot complain as regards the number of works, really important works, inscribed to me. There are so many—by Chausson (his symphony), Ropartz, Dubois (his sonata—one of the best after Franck), d'Indy (the *Istar* variations and other works), Gabriel Fauré (the *Quintet*), Debussy (the *Quartet*)! There are more than I can recall at the moment—violin sonatas, symphonic music, chamber-music, choral works, compositions of every kind!

"Debussy, as you know, wrote practically nothing originally for the violin and piano—with the exception, perhaps, of a work published by Durand during his last illness. Yet he came very near writing something for me. Fifteen years ago he told me he was composing a 'Nocturne' for me. I went off on a concert tour and was away a long time. When I returned to Paris I wrote to Debussy to find out what had become of my 'Nocturne.' And he replied that, somehow, it had shaped itself up for orchestra instead of a violin solo. It is one of the *Trois Nocturnes* for orchestra. Perhaps one reason why so much has been inscribed to me is the fact that as an interpreting artist, I have never cultivated a 'specialty.' I have played everything from Bach to Debussy, for real art should be international!"

Ysaye himself has an almost marvelous right-arm and finger-board control, which enables him to produce at will the finest and most subtle tonal nuances in all bowings. Then, too, he overcomes the most intricate mechanical problems with seemingly effortless ease. And his tone has well been called "golden." His own definition of tone is worth recording. He says it should be "In music what the heart suggests, and the soul expresses!"

THE TOOLS OF VIOLIN MASTERY

"With regard to mechanism," Ysaye continued, "at the present day the tools of violin mastery, of expression, technique, mechanism, are far more necessary than in days gone by. In fact they are indispensable, if the spirit is to express itself without restraint. And the greater mechanical command one has the less noticeable it becomes. All that suggests effort, awkwardness, difficulty, repels the listener, who more than anything else delights in a singing violin tone. Vieuxtemps often said: *Pas de trait pour le trait—chantez, chantez!* (Not runs for the sake of runs—sing, sing!)

"Too many of the technicians of the present day no longer sing. Their difficulties—they surmount them more or less happily; but the effect is too apparent, and though, at times, the listener may be astonished, he can never be charmed. Agile fin- gers, sure of themselves, and a perfect bow stroke are essentials; and they must be supremely able to carry along the rhythm and poetic action the artist desires. Mechanism becomes, if anything, more accessible in proportion as its domain is enriched by new formulas. The violinist of today commands far greater technical resources than did his predecessors. Paganini is accessible to nearly all players: Vieuxtemps no longer offers the difficulties he did thirty years ago. Yet the wood-wind, brass and even the string instruments subsist in a measure on the heritage transmitted by the masters of the past. I often feel that violin teaching today endeavors to develop the æsthetic sense at too early a stage. And in devoting itself to the *head* it forgets the *hands,* with the result that the young soldiers of the violinistic army, full of ardor and courage, are ill equipped for the great battle of art.

"In this connection there exists an excellent set of *Études-Caprices* by E. Chaumont, which offer the advanced student new elements and formulas of development. Though in some of them 'the frame is too large for the picture,' and though difficult from a violinistic point of view, 'they lie admirably well up the neck,' to use one of Vieuxtemps's expressions, and I take pleasure in calling attention to them.

"When I said that the string instruments, including the violin, subsist in a measure on the heritage transmitted by the masters of the past, I spoke with special regard to technique. Since Vieuxtemps there has been hardly one new passage written for the violin; and this has retarded the development of its technique. In the case of the piano, men like Godowsky have created a new technique for their instrument; but although Saint-Saëns, Bruch, Lalo and others have in their works endowed the violin with much beautiful music, music itself was their first concern, and not music for the violin. There are no more concertos written for the solo flute, trombone, etc.—as a result there is no new technical material added to the resources of these instruments.

"In a way the same holds good of the violin—new works conceived only from the musical point of view bring about the stagnation of technical discovery, the invention of new passages, of novel harmonic wealth of combination is not encouraged. And a violinist owes it to himself to exploit the great possibilities of his own instrument. I have tried to find new technical ways and means of expression in my own compositions. For example, I have written a *Divertiment* for violin and orchestra in which I believe I have embodied new thoughts and ideas, and have attempted to give violin technique a broader scope of life and vigor.

"In the days of Viotti and Rode the harmonic possibilities were more limited—they had only a few chords, and hardly any chords of the ninth. But now harmonic material for the development of a new violin technique is there: I have some violin studies, in ms., which I may publish some day, devoted to that end. I am always somewhat hesitant about publishing—there are many things I might publish, but I have seen so much brought out that was banal, poor, unworthy, that I have always been inclined to mistrust the value of my own creations rather than fall into the same error. We have the scale of Debussy and his successors to draw upon, their new chords and successions of fourths and fifths—for new technical formulas are always evolved out of and follow after new harmonic discoveries—though there is as yet no violin method which gives a fingering for the whole-tone scale. Perhaps we will have to wait until Kreisler or I will have written one which makes plain the new flowering of technical beauty and æsthetic development which it brings the violin.

"As to teaching violin, I have never taught violin in the generally accepted sense of the phrase. But at Godinne, where I usually spent my summers when in Europe, I gave a kind of traditional course in the works of Vieuxtemps, Wieniawski and other masters to some forty or fifty artist-students who would gather there—the same course I look forward to giving in Cincinnati, to a master class of very advanced pupils. This was and will be a labor of love, for the compositions of Vieuxtemps and Wieniawski especially are so inspiring and yet, as a rule, they are so badly played—without grandeur or beauty, with no thought of the traditional interpretation—that they seem the piecework of technique factories!

VIOLIN MASTERY

"When I take the whole history of the violin into account I feel that the true inwardness of 'Violin Mastery' is best expressed by a kind of threefold group of great artists. First, in the order of romantic expression, we have a trinity made up of Corelli, Viotti and Vieuxtemps. Then there is a trinity of mechanical perfection, composed of Locatelli, Tartini and Paganini or, a more modern equivalent, César Thomson, Kubelik and Burmeister. And, finally, what I might call in the order of lyric expression, a quartet comprising Ysaye, Thibaud, Mischa Elman and Sametini of Chicago, the last-named a wonderfully fine artist of the lyric or singing type. Of course there are qualifications to be made. Locatelli was not altogether an exponent of technique. And many other fine artists besides those mentioned share the characteristics of those in the various groups. Yet, speaking in a general way, I believe that these groups of attainment might be said to sum up what 'Violin Mastery' really is. And a violin master? He must be a violinist, a thinker, a poet, a human being, he must have known hope, love, passion and despair, he must have run the gamut of the emotions in order to express them all in his playing. He must play his violin as Pan played his flute!"

In conclusion Ysaye sounded a note of warning for the too ambitious young student and player. "If Art is to progress, the technical and mechanical element must not, of course, be neglected. But a boy of eighteen cannot expect to express that to which the serious student of thirty, the man who has actually lived, can give voice. If the violinist's art is truly a great art, it cannot come to fruition in the artist's 'teens. His accomplishment then is no more than a promise—a promise which finds its realization in and by life itself. Yet Americans have the brains as well as the spiritual endowment necessary to understand and appreciate beauty in a high degree. They can already point with pride to violinists who emphatically deserve to be called artists, and another quarter-century of artistic striving may well bring them into the front rank of violinistic achievement!"

LEOPOLD AUER

A METHOD WITHOUT SECRETS

When that celebrated laboratory of budding musical genius, the Petrograd Conservatory, closed its doors indefinitely owing to the disturbed political conditions of Russia, the famous violinist and teacher Professor Leopold Auer decided to pay the visit to the United States which had so repeatedly been urged on him by his friends and pupils. His fame, owing to such heralds as Efrem Zimbalist, Mischa Elman, Kathleen Parlow, Eddy Brown, Francis MacMillan, and more recently Sascha Heifetz, Toscha Seidel, and Max Rosen, had long since preceded him; and the reception accorded him in this country, as a soloist and one of the greatest exponents and teachers of his instrument, has been one justly due to his authority and preeminence.

It was not easy to have a heart-to-heart talk with the Master anent his art, since every minute of his time was precious. Yet ushered into his presence, the writer discovered that he had laid aside for the moment other preoccupations, and was amiably responsive to all questions, once their object had been disclosed. Naturally, the first and burning question in the case of so celebrated a pedagogue was: "How do you form such wonderful artists? What is the secret of your method?"

A METHOD WITHOUT SECRETS

"I know," said Professor Auer, "that there is a theory somewhat to the effect that I make a few magic passes with the bow by way of illustration and—*presto*—you have a Zimbalist or a

8

LEOPOLD AUER

Heifetz! But the truth is I have no method—unless you want to call purely natural lines of development, based on natural principles, a method—and so, of course, there is no secret about my teaching. The one great point I lay stress on in teaching is never to kill the individuality of my various pupils. Each pupil has his own inborn aptitudes, his own personal qualities as regards tone and interpretation. I always have made an individual study of each pupil, and given each pupil individual treatment. And always, always I have encouraged them to develop freely in their own way as regards inspiration and ideals, so long as this was not contrary to æsthetic principles and those of my art. My idea has always been to help bring out what nature has already given, rather than to use dogma to force a student's natural inclinations into channels I myself might prefer. And another great principle in my teaching, one which is productive of results, is to demand as much as possible of the pupil. Then he will give you something!

"Of course the whole subject of violin teaching is one that I look at from the standpoint of the teacher who tries to make what is already excellent perfect from the musical and artistic standpoint. I insist on a perfected technical development in every pupil who comes to me. Art begins where technique ends. There can be no real art development before one's technique is firmly established. And a great deal of technical work has to be done before the great works of violin literature, the sonatas and concertos, may be approached. In Petrograd my own assistants, who were familiar with my ideas, prepared my pupils for me. And in my own experience I have found that one cannot teach by word, by the spoken explanation, alone. If I have a point to make I explain it; but if my explanation fails to explain I take my violin and bow, and clear up the matter beyond any doubt. The word lives, it is true, but often the word must be materialized by action so that its meaning is clear. There are always things which the pupil must be shown literally, though explanation should always supplement illustration. I studied with Joachim as a boy of sixteen—it was before 1866, when there was still a kingdom of Hanover in existence—and Joachim always illustrated his meaning with bow and fiddle. But he never explained the technical side of what he illustrated. Those more advanced understood without verbal comment; yet there were some who did not.

"As regards the theory that you can tell who a violinist's teacher is by the way in which he plays, I do not believe in it. I do not believe that you can tell an Auer pupil by the manner in which he plays. And I am proud of it since it shows that my pupils have profited by my encouragement of individual development, and that they become genuine artists, each with a personality of his own, instead of violinistic automats, all bearing a marked family resemblance."

Questioned as to how his various pupils reflected different phases of his teaching ideals, Professor Auer mentioned that he had long since given over passing final decisions on his pupils. "I could express no such opinions without unconsciously implying comparisons. And so few comparisons really compare! Then, too, mine would be merely an individual opinion. Therefore, as has been my custom for years, I will continue to leave any ultimate decisions regarding my pupils' playing to the public and the press."

HOURS OF PRACTICE

"How long should the advanced pupil practice?" Professor Auer was asked. "The right kind of practice is not a matter of hours," he replied. "Practice should represent the utmost concentration of brain. It is better to play with concentration for two hours than to practice eight without. I should say that four hours would be a good maximum practice time—I never ask more of my pupils—and that during each minute of the time the brain be as active as the fingers.

NATIONALITY VERSUS THE CONSERVATORY SYSTEM

"I think there is more value in the idea of a national conservatory than in the idea of nationality as regards violin playing. No matter what his birthplace, there is only one way in which a student can become an artist—and that is to have a teacher who can teach! In Europe the best teachers are to be found in the great national conservatories. Thibaud, Ysaye—artists of the highest type—are products of the conservatory system, with its splendid teachers. So is Kreisler, one of the greatest artists, who studied in Vienna and Paris. Eddy Brown, the brilliant American violinist, finished at the Budapest Conservatory. In the Paris Conservatory the number of pupils in a class is strictly limited; and from these pupils each professor chooses the very best—who may not be able to pay for their course—for free instruction. At the Petrograd Conservatory, where Wieniawski preceded me, there were hundreds of free scholarships available. If a really big talent came along he always had his opportunity. We took and taught those less talented at the Conservatory in order to be able to give scholarships to the deserving of limited means. In this way no real violinistic genius, whom poverty might otherwise have kept from ever realizing his dreams, was deprived of his chance in life. Among the pupils there in my class, having scholarships, were Kathleen Parlow, Elman, Zimbalist, Heifetz and Seidel.

VIOLIN MASTERY

"'Violin Mastery'? To me it represents the sum total of accomplishment on the part of those who live in the history of the Art. All those who may have died long since, yet the memory of whose work and whose creations still lives, are the true masters of the violin, and its mastery is the record of their accomplishment. As a child I remember the well-known composers of the day were Marschner, Hiller, Nicolai and others— yet most of what they have written has been forgotten. On the other hand there are Tartini, Nardini, Paganini, Kreutzer, Dont and Rode—they still live; and so do Ernst, Sarasate, Vieuxtemps and Wieniawski. Joachim (incidentally the only great German violinist of whom I know—and he was a Hungarian!), though he had but few great pupils, and composed but little, will always be remembered because he, together with David, gave violin virtuosity a nobler trend, and introduced a higher ideal in the music played for violin. It is men such as these who always will remain violin 'masters,' just as 'Violin Mastery' is defined by what they have done."

THE BACH VIOLIN SONATAS
AND OTHER COMPOSITIONS

Replying to a question as to the value of the Bach violin sonatas, Professor Auer said: "My pupils always have to play Bach. I have published my own revision of them with a New York house. The most impressive thing about these Bach solo sonatas is they do not need an accompaniment: one feels it would be superfluous. Bach composed so rapidly, he wrote with such ease, that it would have been no trouble for him to supply one had he felt it necessary. But he did not, and he was right. And they still must be played as he has written them. We have the 'modern' orchestra, the 'modern' piano, but, thank heaven, no 'modern' violin! Such indications as I have made in my edition with regard to bowing, fingering, *nuances* of expression, are more or less in accord with the spirit of the times; but not a single note that Bach has written has been changed. The sonatas are technically among the most difficult things written for the violin, excepting Ernst and Paganini. Not that they are hard in a modern way: Bach knew nothing of harmonics, *pizzicati,* scales in octaves and tenths. But his counterpoint, his fugues—to play them well when the principal theme is sometimes in the outer voices, sometimes in the inner voices, or moving from one to the other—is supremely difficult! In the last sonatas there is a larger number of small movements—but this does not make them any easier to play.

"I have also edited the Beethoven sonatas together with Rudolph Ganz. He worked at the piano parts in New York, while I studied and revised the violin parts in Petrograd and Norway, where I spent my summers during the war. There was not so much to do," said Professor Auer modestly, "a little fingering, some bowing indications and not much else. No reviser needs to put any indications for *nuance* and shading in Beethoven. He was quite able to attend to all that himself. There is no composer who shows such refinement of *nuance*. You need only to take his quartets or these same sonatas to convince yourself of the fact. In my Brahms revisions I have supplied really needed fingerings, bowings, and other indications! Important compositions on which I am now at work include Ernst's fine *Concerto*, Op. 23, the Mozart violin concertos, and Tartini's *Trille du diable*, with a special cadenza for my pupil, Toscha Seidel.

AS REGARDS "PRODIGIES"

"Prodigies?" said Professor Auer. "The word 'prodigy' when applied to some youthful artist is always used with an accent of reproach. Public and critics are inclined to regard them with suspicion. Why? After all, the important thing is not their youth, but their artistry. Examine the history of music—you will discover that any number of great masters, great in the maturity of their genius, were great in its infancy as well. There are Mozart, Beethoven, Liszt, Rubinstein, d'Albert, Hofmann, Scriabin, Wieniawski—they were all 'infant prodigies,' and certainly not in any objectionable sense. Not that I wish to claim that every *prodigy* necessarily becomes a great master. That does not always follow. But I believe that a musical prodigy, instead of being regarded with suspicion, has a right to be looked upon as a striking example of a pronounced natural predisposition for musical art. Of course, full mental development of artistic power must come as a result of the maturing processes of life itself. But I firmly believe that every prodigy represents a valuable musical phenomenon, one deserving of the keenest interest and encouragement. It does not seem right to me that when the art of the prodigy is incontestably great, that the mere fact of his youth should serve as an excuse to look upon him with prejudice, and even with a certain degree of distrust."

EDDY BROWN

HUBAY AND AUER: TECHNIQUE:
HINTS TO THE STUDENT

Notwithstanding the fact that Eddy Brown was born in Chicago, Ill., and that he is so great a favorite with concert audiences in the land of his birth, the gifted violinist hesitates to qualify himself as a strictly "American" violinist. As he express-es it: "Musically I was altogether educated in Europe—I never studied here, because I left this country at the age of seven, and only returned a few years ago. So I would not like to be placed in the position of claiming anything under false pretenses!

HUBAY AND AUER: SOME COMPARISONS

"With whom did I study? With two famous masters; by a strange coincidence both Hungarians. First with Jenö Hubay, at the National Academy of Music in Budapest, later with Leopold Auer in Petrograd. Hubay had been a pupil of Vieuxtemps in Brussels, and is a justly celebrated teacher, very thorough and painstaking in explaining to his pupils how to do things; but the great difference between Hubay and Auer is that while Hubay tells a student how to do things, Auer, a temperamental teacher, literally drags out of him whatever there is in him, awakening latent powers he never knew he possessed. Hubay is a splendid builder of virtuosity, and has a fine sense for phrasing. For a year and a half I worked at nothing but studies with him, giving special attention to technique. He did not believe in giving too much time to left hand development, when without adequate bow technique finger facility is useless. Here he was in accord

15

with Auer, in fact with every teacher seriously deserving of the name. Hubay was a first-class pedagogue, and under his instruction one could not help becoming a well-balanced and musicianly player. But there is a higher ideal in violin playing than mere correctness, and Auer is an inspiring teacher. Hubay has written some admirable studies, notably twelve studies for the right hand, though he never stressed technique too greatly. On the other hand, Auer's most notable contributions to violin literature are his revisions of such works as the Bach sonatas, the Tchaikovsky *Concerto,* etc. In a way it points the difference in their mental attitude: Hubay more concerned with the technical educational means, one which cannot be overlooked; Auer more interested in the interpretative, artistic educational end, which has always claimed his attention. Hubay personally was a *grand seigneur,* a multi-millionaire, and married to an Hungarian countess. He had a fine ear for phrasing, could improvise most interesting violin accompaniments to whatever his pupils played, and beside Rode, Kreutzer and Fiorillo I studied the concertos and other repertory works with him. Then there were the conservatory lessons! Attendance at a European conservatory is very broadening musically. Not only does the individual violin pupil, for example, profit by listening to his colleagues play in class: he also studies theory, musical history, the piano, *ensemble* playing, chamber-music and orchestra. I was concertmaster of the conservatory orchestra while studying with Hubay. There should be a national conservatory of music in this country; music in general would advance more rapidly. And it would help teach American students to approach the art of violin playing from the right point of view. As it is, too many want to study abroad under some renowned teacher not, primarily, with the idea of becoming great artists; but in the hope of drawing great future commercial dividends from an initial financial investment. In Art the financial should always be a secondary consideration.

"It stands to reason that no matter how great a student's gifts may be, he can profit by study with a great teacher. This, I think, applies to all. After I had already appeared in concert at Albert Hall, London, in 1909, where I played the Beethoven *Concerto* with orchestra, I decided to study with Auer. When I first came to him he wanted to know why I did so, and after hearing me play, told me that I did not need any lessons from him. But I knew that there was a certain 'something' which I wished to add to my violinistic make-up, and instinctively felt that he alone could give me what I wanted. I soon found that in many essentials his ideas coincided with those of Hubay. But I also discovered that Auer made me develop my individuality unconsciously, placing no undue restrictions whatsoever upon my manner of expression, barring, of course, unmusicianly tendencies. When he has a really talented pupil the Professor gives him of his best. I never gave a thought to technique while I studied with him—the great things were a singing tone, bowing, interpretation! I studied Brahms and Beethoven, and though Hubay always finished with the Bach sonatas, I studied them again carefully with Auer.

TECHNIQUE: SOME HINTS TO THE STUDENT

"At the bottom of all technique lies the scale. And scale practice is the ladder by means of which all must climb to higher proficiency. Scales, in single tones and intervals, thirds, sixths, octaves, tenths, with the incidental changes of position, are the foundation of technique. They should be practiced slowly, always with the development of tone in mind, and not too long a time at any one session. No one can lay claim to a perfected technique who has not mastered the scale. Better a good tone, even though a hundred mistakes be made in producing it, than a tone that is poor, thin and without quality. I find the Singer *Fingerübungen* are excellent for muscular development in scale work, for imparting the great strength which is necessary for the fingers to have; and the Kreutzer *études* are indispensable. To secure an absolute *legato* tone, a true singing tone on the violin, one should play scales with a perfectly well sustained and steady bow, in whole notes, slowly and *mezzo-forte*, taking care that each note is clear and pure, and that its volume does not vary during the stroke. The quality of tone must be equalized, and each whole note should be 'sung' with a single bowing. The change from up-bow to down-bow and *vice versa* should be made without a break, exclusively through skillful manipulation of the wrist. To accomplish this unbroken change of bow one should cultivate a loose wrist, and do special work at the extreme ends, nut and tip.

"The *vibrato* is a great tone beautifier. Too rapid or too slow a *vibrato* defeats the object desired. There is a happy medium of *tempo,* rather faster than slower, which gives the best results. Carl Flesch has some interesting theories about vibration which are worth investigating. A slow and a moderately rapid *vibrato, from the wrist,* is best for practice, and the underlying idea while working must be tone, and not fingerwork.

"*Staccato* is one of the less important branches of bow technique. There is a knack in doing it, and it is purely pyrotechnical. *Staccato* passages in quantity are only to be found in solos of the virtuoso type. One never meets with extended *staccato* passages in Beethoven, Brahms, Bruch or Lalo. And the Saint-Saëns's *Violin Concerto,* if I remember rightly, contains but a single *staccato* passage.

"*Spiccato* is a very different matter from *staccato:* violinists as a rule use the middle of the bow for *spiccato:* I use the upper third of the bow, and thus get most satisfactory results, in no matter what *tempo.* This question as to what portion of the bow to use for *spiccato* each violinist must decide for himself, however, through experiment. I have tried both ways and find that by the last mentioned use of the bow I secure quicker, cleaner results. Students while practicing this bowing should take care that the wrist, and never the arm, be used. Hubay has written some very excellent studies for this form of 'springing bow.'

"The trill, when it rolls quickly and evenly, is a trill indeed! I never had any difficulty in acquiring it, and can keep on trilling indefinitely without the slightest unevenness or slackening of speed. Auer himself has assured me that I have a trill that runs on and on without a sign of fatigue or uncertainty. The trill has to be practiced very slowly at first, later with increasing rapidity, and always with a firm pressure of the fingers. It is a very beautiful embellishment, and one much used; one finds it in Beethoven, Mendelssohn, Brahms, etc.

"Double notes never seemed hard to me, but harmonics are not as easily acquired as some of the other violin effects. I advise pressing down the first finger on the strings *inordinately,* especially in the higher positions, when playing artificial harmonics. The higher the fingers ascend on the strings, the more firmly they should press them, otherwise the harmonics are apt to grow shrill and lose in clearness. The majority of students have trouble with their harmonics, because they do not practice them in this way. Of course the quality of the harmonics produced varies with the quality of the strings that produce them. First class strings are an absolute necessity for the production of pure harmonics. Yet in the case of the artist, he himself is held responsible, and not his strings.

"Octaves? Occasionally, as in Auer's transcript of Beethoven's *Dance of the Dervishes,* or in the closing section of the Ernst *Concerto,* when they are used to obtain a certain weird effect, they sound well. But ordinarily, if cleanly played, they sound like one-note successions. In the examples mentioned, the so-called 'fingered octaves,' which are very difficult, are employed. Ordinary octaves are not so troublesome. After all, in octave playing we simply double the notes for the purpose of making them more powerful.

"As regards the playing of tenths, it seems to me that the interval always sounds constrained, and hardly ever euphonious enough to justify its difficulty, especially in rapid passages. Yet Paganini used this awkward interval very freely in his compositions, and one of his *Caprices* is a variation in tenths, which should be played more often than it is, as it is very effective. In this connection change of position, which I have already touched on with regard to scale playing, should be so smooth that it escapes notice. Among special effects the *glissando* is really beautiful when properly done. And this calls for judgment. It might be added, though, that the *glissando* is an effect which should not be overdone. The *portamento*—gliding from one note to another—is also a lovely effect. Its proper and timely application calls for good judgment and sound musical taste.

A SPANISH VIOLIN

"I usually play a 'Strad,' but very often turn to my beautiful 'Guillami,'" said Mr. Brown when asked about his violins. "It is an old Spanish violin, made in Barcelona, in 1728, with a tone

that has a distinct Stradivarius character. In appearance it closely resembles a Guadagnini, and has often been taken for one.
When the dealer of whom I bought it first showed it to me it was
complete—but in four distinct pieces! Kubelik, who was in
Budapest at the time, heard of it and wanted to buy it; but the
dealer, as was only right, did not forget that my offer represented a prior claim, and so I secured it. The Guadagnini, which I
have played in all my concerts here, I am very fond of—it has a
Stradivarius tone rather than the one we usually associate with
the make." Mr. Brown showed the writer his Grancino, a beautiful little instrument about to be sent to the repair shop, since
exposure to the damp atmosphere of the sea-shore had opened
its seams—and the rare and valuable Simon bow, now his, which
had once been the property of Sivori. Mr. Brown has used a wire
E ever since he broke six gut strings in one hour while at Seal
Harbor, Maine. "A wire string, I find, is not only easier to play,
but it has a more brilliant quality of tone than a gut string; and
I am now so accustomed to using a wire E, that I would feel ill
at ease if I did not have one on my instrument. Contrary to general belief, it does not sound 'metallic,' unless the string itself is
of very poor quality.

PROGRAMS

"In making up a recital program I try to arrange it so that the
first half, approximately, may appeal to the more specifically
musical part of my audience, and to the critics. In the second
half I endeavor to remember the general public; at the same
time being careful to include nothing which is not really *musical*. This (Mr. Brown found one of his recent programs on his
desk and handed it to me) represents a logical compromise
between the strictly artistic and the more general taste:"

PROGRAM

I. Beethoven . . . . *Sonata,* Op. 47 (dedicated to Kreutzer)
II. Bruch . . . . *Concerto* (G minor)
III. (a) Beethoven . . . . . *Romance* (in G major)
    (b) Beethoven-Auer . . *Chorus of the Dervishes*
    (c) Brown . . . . *Rondino* (on a Cramer theme)

  (d) Arbos . . . . *Tango*
IV. (a) Kreisler . . . . *La Gitana*
     (Arabo-Spanish Gipsy Dance of the 18th Century)
     (b) Cui . . . . *Orientale*
     (c) Bazzini . . . . *La Ronde des Lutins*

"As you see there are two extended serious works, followed
by two smaller 'groups' of pieces. And these have also been chosen with a view to contrast. The *finale* of the Bruch *Concerto* is
an *allegro energico:* I follow it with a Beethoven *Romance,* a
slow movement. The second group begins with a taking Kreisler
novelty, which is succeeded by another slow number; but one
very effective in its working-up; and I end my program with a
brilliant virtuoso number.

VIOLIN MASTERY

"My own personal conception of 'Violin Mastery,' concluded
Mr. Brown, "might be defined as follows: 'An individual tone
production, or rather tone quality, consummate musicianship in
phrasing and interpretation, ability to rise above all mechanical
and intellectual effort, and finally the power to express that
which is dictated by one's imagination and emotion, with the
same natural simplicity and spontaneity with which the thought
of a really great orator is expressed in the easy, unconstrained
flow of his language.'"

MISCHA ELMAN

LIFE AND COLOR IN INTERPRETATION.
TECHNICAL PHASES

To hear Mischa Elman on the concert platform, to listen to him play, "with all that wealth of tone, emotion and impulse which places him in the very foremost rank of living violinists," should be joy enough for any music lover. To talk with him in his own home, however, gives one a deeper insight into his art as an interpreter; and in the pleasant intimacy of familiar conversation the writer learned much that the serious student of the violin will be interested in knowing.

MANNERISMS IN PLAYING

We all know that Elman, when he plays in public, moves his head, moves his body, sways in time to the music; in a word there are certain mannerisms associated with his playing which critics have on occasion mentioned with grave suspicion, as evidences of sensationalism. Half fearing to insult him by asking whether he was "sincere," or whether his motions were "stage business" carefully rehearsed, as had been implied, I still ventured the question. He laughed boyishly and was evidently much amused.

"No, no," he said. "I do not study up any 'stage business' to help out my playing! I do not know whether I ought to compare myself to a dancer, but the appeal of the dance is in all musical movement. Certain rhythms and musical combinations affect me subconsciously. I suppose the direct influence of the music on me is such that there is a sort of emotional reflex: I move with

Mischa Elman

the music in an unconscious translation of it into gesture. It is all so individual. The French violinists as a rule play very correctly in public, keeping their eye on finger and bow. And this appeals to me strongly in theory. In practice I seem to get away from it. It is a matter of temperament I presume. I am willing to believe I'm not graceful, but then—I do not know whether I move or do not move! Some of my friends have spoken of it to me at various times, so I suppose I do move, and sway and all the rest; but any movements of the sort must be unconscious, for I myself know nothing of them. And the idea that they are 'prepared' as 'stage effects' is delightful!" And again Elman laughed.

LIFE AND COLOR IN INTERPRETATION

"For that matter," he continued, "every real artist has some mannerisms when playing, I imagine. Yet more than mannerisms are needed to impress an American audience. Life and color in interpretation are the true secrets of great art. And beauty of interpretation depends, first of all, on variety of color. Technique is, after all, only secondary. No matter how well played a composition be, its performance must have color, *nuance,* movement, life! Each emotional mood of the moment must be fully expressed, and if it is its appeal is sure. I remember when I once played for Don Manuel, the young ex-king of Portugal, in London, I had an illustration of the fact. He was just a pathetic boy, very democratic, and personally very likeable. He was somewhat neglected at the time, for it is well known and not altogether unnatural, that royalty securely established finds 'kings in exile' a bit embarrassing. Don Manuel was a music-lover, and especially fond of Bach. I had had long talks with the young king at various times, and my sympathies had been aroused in his behalf. On the evening of which I speak I played a Chopin *Nocturne,* and I know that into my playing there went some of my feeling for the pathos of the situation of this young stranger in a strange land, of my own age, eating the bitter bread of exile. When I had finished, the Marchioness of Ripon touched my arm: 'Look at the King!' she whispered. Don Manuel had been moved to tears.

"Of course the purely mechanical must always be dominated

by the artistic personality of the player. Yet technique is also an important part of interpretation: knowing exactly how long to hold a bow, the most delicate inflections of its pressure on the strings. There must be perfect sympathy also with the composer's thought; his spirit must stand behind the personality of the artist. In the case of certain famous compositions, like the Beethoven *Concerto,* for instance, this is so well established that the artist, and never the composer, is held responsible if it is not well played. But too rigorous an adherence to 'tradition' in playing is also an extreme. I once played privately for Joachim in Berlin: it was the Bach *Chaconne.* Now the edition I used was a standard one: and Joachim was extremely reverential as regards traditions. Yet he did not hesitate to indicate some changes which he thought should be made in the version of an authoritative edition, because 'they sounded better.' And 'How does it sound?' is really the true test of all interpretation."

ABSOLUTE PITCH THE FIRST ESSENTIAL
OF A PERFECTED TECHNIQUE

"What is the fundamental of a perfected violin technique?" was a natural question at this point. "Absolute pitch, first of all," replied Elman promptly. "Many a violinist plays a difficult passage, sounding every note; and yet it sounds out of tune. The first and second movements of the Beethoven *Concerto* have no double-stops; yet they are extremely difficult to play. Why? Because they call for absolute pitch: they must be played in perfect tune so that each tone stands out in all its fullness and clarity like a rock in the sea. And without a fundamental control of pitch such a master work will always be beyond the violinist's reach. Many a player has the facility; but without perfect intonation he can never attain the highest perfection. On the other hand, any one who can play a single phrase in absolute pitch has the first and great essential. Few artists, not barring some of the greatest, play with perfect intonation. Its control depends first of all on the ear. And a sensitive ear finds differences and shading; it bids the violinist play a trifle sharper, a trifle flatter, according to the general harmonic color of the accompaniment; it leads him to observe a difference, when the harmonic atmosphere demands it, between a C sharp in the key of E major and a D flat in the same key.

TECHNICAL PHASES

"Every player finds some phases of technique easy and others difficult. For instance, I have never had to work hard for quality of tone—when I wish to get certain color effects they come: I have no difficulty in expressing my feelings, my emotions in tone. And in a technical way *spiccato* bowing, which many find so hard, has always been easy to me. I have never had to work for it. Double-stops, on the contrary, cost me hours of intensive work before I played them with ease and facility. What did I practice? Scales in double-stops—they give color and variety to tone. And I gave up a certain portion of my regular practice time to passages from concertos and sonatas. There is wonderful work in double-stops in the Ernst *Concerto* and in the Paganini *Études*, for instance. With octaves and tenths I have never had any trouble: I have a broad hand and a wide stretch, which accounts for it, I suppose.

"Then there are harmonics, flageolets—I have never been able to understand why they should be considered so difficult! They should not be white, colorless; but call for just as much color as any other tones (and any one who has heard Mischa Elman play harmonics knows that this is no mere theory on his part). I never think of harmonics as 'harmonics,' but try to give them just as much expressive quality as the notes of any other register. The mental attitude should influence their production—too many violinists think of them only as incidental to pyrotechnical display.

"And fingering? Fingering in general seems to me to be an individual matter. A concert artist may use a certain fingering for a certain passage which no pupil should use, and be entirely justified if he can thus secure a certain effect.

"I do not—speaking out of my own experience—believe much in methods: and never to the extent that they be allowed to kill the student's individuality. A clear, clean tone should always be the ideal of his striving. And to that end he must see that the up and down bows in a passage like the following from

the Bach *Sonata in A minor* (and Mr. Elman hastily jotted down
the subjoined) are absolutely even, and of the same length,

played with the same strength and length of bow, otherwise the
notes are swallowed. In light *spiccato* and *staccato* the detached
notes should be played always with a single stroke of the bow.
Some players, strange to say, find *staccato* notes more difficult
to play at a moderate tempo than fast. I believe it to be altogether a matter of control—if proper control be there the
tempo makes no difference. Wieniawski, I have read, could only
play his *staccati* at a high rate of speed. *Spiccato* is generally
held to be more difficult than *staccato;* yet I myself find it
easier.

PROPORTION IN PRACTICE

"To influence a clear, singing tone with the left hand, to
phrase it properly with the bow hand, is most important. And it
is a matter of proportion. Good phrasing is spoiled by an ugly
tone: a beautiful singing tone loses meaning if improperly
phrased. When the student has reached a certain point of technical development, technique must be a secondary—yet not
neglected—consideration, and he should devote himself to the
production of a good tone. Many violinists have missed their
career by exaggerated attention to either bow or violin hand.
Both hands must be watched at the same time. And the question of proportion should always be kept in mind in practicing
studies and passages: pressure of fingers and pressure of bow
must be equalized, coordinated. The teacher can only do a certain amount: the pupil must do the rest.

AUER AS A TEACHER

"Take Auer for example. I may call myself the first real exponent of his school, in the sense of making his name widely
known. Auer is a great teacher, and leaves much to the individuality of his pupils. He first heard me play at the Imperial Music
School in Odessa, and took me to Petrograd to study with him,

which I did for a year and four months. And he could accomplish wonders! That one year he had a little group of four pupils each one better than the other—a very stimulating situation for all of them. There was a magnetism about him: he literally hypnotized his pupils into doing better than their best—though in some cases it was evident that once the support of his magnetic personality was withdrawn, the pupil fell back into the level from which he had been raised for the time being.

"Yet Auer respected the fact that temperamentally I was not responsive to this form of appeal. He gave me of his best. I never practiced more than two or three hours a day—just enough to keep fresh. Often I came to my lesson unprepared, and he would have me play things—sonatas, concertos—which I had not touched for a year or more. He was a severe critic, but always a just one.

"I can recall how proud I was when he sent me to beautiful music-loving Helsingfors, in Finland—where all seems to be bloodshed and confusion now—to play a recital in his own stead on one occasion, and how proud he was of my success. Yet Auer had his little peculiarities. I have read somewhere that the great fencing-masters of the sixteenth and seventeenth centuries were very jealous of the secrets of their famous feints and *ripostes,* and only confided them to favorite pupils who promised not to reveal them. Auer had his little secrets, too, with which he was loth to part. When I was to make my *début* in Berlin, I remember, he was naturally enough interested— since I was his pupil—in my scoring a triumph. And he decided to part with some of his treasured technical thrusts and parries. And when I was going over the Tchaikovsky *D minor Concerto* (which I was to play), he would select a passage and say: 'Now I'll play this for you. If you catch it, well and good; if not it is your own fault!' I am happy to say that I did not fail to 'catch' his meaning on any occasion. Auer really has a wonderful intellect, and some secrets well worth knowing. That he is so great an artist himself on the instrument is the more remarkable, since physically he was not exceptionally favored. Often, when he saw me, he'd say with a sigh: 'Ah, if I only had your hand!'

"Auer was a great virtuoso player. He held a unique place in the Imperial Ballet. You know in many of the celebrated ballets, Tchaikovsky's for instance, there occur beautiful and difficult solos for the violin. They call for an artist of the first rank, and Auer was accustomed to play them in Petrograd. In Russia it was considered a decided honor to be called upon to play one of those ballet solos; but in London it was looked on as something quite incidental. I remember when Diaghilev presented Tchaikovsky's *Lac des Cygnes* in London, the Grand-Duke Andrew Vladimirev (who had heard me play), an amiable young boy, and a patron of the arts, requested me— and at that time the request of a Romanov was still equivalent to a command—to play the violin solos which accompany the love scenes. It was not exactly easy, since I had to play and watch dancers and conductor at the same time. Yet it was a novelty for London, however; everybody was pleased and the Grand-Duke presented me with a handsome diamond pin as an acknowledgment.

VIOLIN MASTERY

"You ask me what I understand by 'Violin Mastery'? Well, it seems to me that the artist who can present anything he plays as a distinct picture, in every detail, framing the composer's idea in the perfect beauty of his plastic rendering, with absolute truth of color and proportion—he is the artist who deserves to be called a master!

"Of course, the instrument the artist uses is an important factor in making it possible for him to do his best. My violin? It is an authentic Strad—dated 1722. I bought it of Willy Burmester in London. You see he did not care much for it. The German style of playing is not calculated to bring out the tone beauty, the quality of the old Italian fiddles. I think Burmester had forced the tone, and it took me some time to make it mellow and truly responsive again, but now . . ." Mr. Elman beamed. It was evident he was satisfied with his instrument. "As to strings," he continued, "I never use wire strings—they have no color, no quality!

WHAT TO STUDY AND HOW

"For the advanced student there is a wealth of study material. No one ever wrote more beautiful violin music than Handel, so rich in invention, in harmonic fullness. In Beethoven there are more ideas than tone—but such ideas! Schubert—all genuine, spontaneous! Bach is so gigantic that the violin often seems inadequate to express him. That is one reason why I do not play more Bach in public.

"The study of a sonata or concerto should entirely absorb the attention of the student to such a degree that, as he is able to play it, it has become a part of him. He should be able to play it as though it were an improvisation—of course without doing violence to the composer's idea. If he masters the composition in the way it should be mastered it becomes a portion of himself. Before I even take up my violin I study a piece thoroughly in score. I read and reread it until I am at home with the composer's thought, and its musical balance and proportion. Then, when I begin to play it, its salient points are already memorized, and the practicing gives me a kind of photographic reflex of detail. After I have not played a number for a long time it fades from my memory—like an old negative—but I need only go over it once or twice to have a clear mnemonic picture of it once more.

TRANSCRIPTIONS

"Yes, I believe in transcriptions for the violin—with certain provisos," said Mr. Elman, in reply to another question. "First of all the music to be transcribed must lend itself naturally to the instrument. Almost any really good melodic line, especially a *cantilena,* will sound with a fitting harmonic development. Violinists of former days like Spohr, Rode and Paganini were more intent on composing music *out of the violin!* The modern idea lays stress first of all on the *idea* in music. In transcribing I try to forget I am a violinist, in order to form a perfect picture of the musical idea—its violinistic development must be a natural, subconscious working-out. If you will look at some of my recent transcripts—the Albaniz *Tango,* the negro melody *Deep*

River and Amani's fine *Orientale*—you will see what I mean. They are conceived as pictures—I have not tried to analyze too much—and while so conceiving them their free harmonic background shapes itself for me without strain or effort.

A REMINISCENCE OF COLONNE

"Conductors with whom I have played? There are many: Hans Richter, who was a master of the baton; Nikisch, one of the greatest in conducting the orchestral accompaniment to a violin solo number; Colonne of Paris, and many others. I had an amusing experience with Colonne once. He brought his orchestra to Russia while I was with Auer, and was giving a concert at Pavlovsk, a summer resort near Petrograd. Colonne had a perfect horror of 'infant prodigies,' and Auer had arranged for me to play with his orchestra without telling him my age—I was eleven at the time. When Colonne saw me, violin in hand, ready to step on the stage, he drew himself up and said with emphasis: 'I play with a prodigy! Never!' Nothing could move him, and I had to play to a piano accompaniment. After he had heard me play, though, he came over to me and said: 'The best apology I can make for what I said is to ask you to do me the honor of playing with the *Orchestre Colonne* in Paris.' He was as good as his word. Four months later I went to Paris and played the Mendelssohn *Concerto* for him with great success."

SAMUEL GARDNER

TECHNIQUE AND MUSICIANSHIP

Samuel Gardner, though born in Jelisavetgrad, Cherson province, in Southern Russia, in 1891, is to all intents and purposes an American, since his family, fleeing the tyranny of an Imperialistic regime of "pogroms" and "Black Hundreds," brought him to this country when a mere child; and here in the United States he has become, to quote Richard Aldrich, "the serious and accomplished artist," whose work on the concert stage has given such pleasure to lovers of violin music at its best. The young violinist, who in the course of the same week had just won two prizes in composition—the Pulitzer Prize (Columbia) for a string quartet, and the Loeb Prize for a symphonic poem— was amiably willing to talk of his study experience for the benefit of other students.

CHARLES MARTIN LOEFFLER
AND FELIX WINTERNITZ AS TEACHERS

"I took up the study of the violin at the age of seven, and when I was nine I went to Charles Martin Loeffler and really began to work seriously. Loeffler was a very strict teacher and very exacting, but he achieved results, for he had a most original way of making his points clear to the student. He started off with the Sevčik studies, laying great stress on the proper finger articulation. And he taught me absolute smoothness in change of position when crossing the strings. For instance, in the second book of Sevčik's *Technical Exercises,* in the third exercise, the bow crosses from G to A, and from D to E, leaving a string between in each crossing. Well, I simply could not manage to get to the second string to be played without the string in between sounding! Loeffler showed me what every good fiddler *must* learn to do: to leap from the end of the down-bow to the up-bow and *vice versa* and then hesitate the fraction of a moment, thus securing a smooth, clean-cut tone, without any vibration of the intermediate string. Loeffler never gave a pupil any rest until he came up to his requirements. I know when I played the seventh and eighth Kreutzer studies for him—they are trill studies—he said: 'You trill like an electric bell, but not fast enough!' And he kept at me to speed up my tempo without loss of clearness or tone-volume, until I could do justice to a rapid trill. It is a great quality in a teacher to be literally able to *enforce* the pupil's progress in certain directions; for though the latter may not appreciate it at the time, later on he is sure to do so. I remember once when he was trying to explain the perfect *crescendo* to me, fire-engine bells began to ring in the distance, the sound gradually drawing nearer the house in Charles Street where I was taking my lesson. 'There you have it!' Loeffler cried: 'There's your ideal *crescendo!* Play it like that and I will be satisfied!' I remained with Loeffler a year and a half, and when he went to Paris began to study with Felix Winternitz.

"Felix Winternitz was a teacher who allowed his pupils to develop individuality. 'I care nothing for theories,' he used to say, 'so long as I can see something original in your work!' He attached little importance to the theory of technique, but a great deal to technical development along individual lines. And he always encouraged me to express myself freely, within my limitations, stressing the musical side of my work. With him I played through the concertos which, after a time, I used for technical material, since every phase of technique and bowing is covered in these great works. I was only fifteen when I left Winternitz and still played by instinct rather than intellectually. I still used my bow arm somewhat stiffly, and did not think much about phrasing. I instinctively phrased whatever the music itself made clear to me, and what I did not understand I merely played.

KNEISEL'S TEACHING METHODS

"But when I came to Franz Kneisel, my last teacher, I began

to work with my mind. Kneisel showed me that I had to think when I played. At first I did not realize why he kept at me so insistently about phrasing, interpretation, the exact observance of expression marks; but eventually it dawned on me that he was teaching me to read a soul into each composition I studied.

"I practiced hard, from four to five hours a day. Fortunately, as regards technical equipment, I was ready for Kneisel's instruction. The first thing he gave me to study was, not a brilliant virtuoso piece, but the Bach *Concerto in E major,* and then the Viotti concerto. In the beginning, until Kneisel showed me, I did not know what to do with them. This was music whose notes in themselves were easy, and whose difficulties were all of an individual order. But intellectual analysis, interpretation, are Kneisel's great points. A strict teacher, I worked with him for five years, the most remarkable years of all my violin study.

"Kneisel knows how to develop technical perfection without using technical exercises. I had already played the Mendelssohn, Bruch and Lalo concertos with Winternitz, and these I now restudied with Kneisel. In interpretation he makes clear every phrase in its relation to every other phrase and the movement as a whole. And he insists on his pupils studying theory and composition—something I had formerly not been inclined to take seriously.

"Some teachers are satisfied if the student plays his *notes* correctly, in a general way. With Kneisel the very least detail, a trill, a scale, has to be given its proper tone-color and dynamic shading in absolute proportion with the balancing harmonies. This trill, in the first movement of the Beethoven *Concerto*—[and Mr. Gardner jotted it down]

Kneisel kept me at during the entire lesson, till I was able to adjust its tone-color and *nuances* to the accompanying harmony. Then, though many teachers do not know it, it is a tradition in the orchestra to make a *diminuendo* in the sixth measure, before the change of key to C major, and this *diminuendo* should, of course, be observed by the solo instrument as well. Yet you will hear well-known artists play the trill throughout with a loud, brilliant tone and no dynamic change!

"Kneisel makes it a point to have all his pupils play chamber music because of its truly broadening influence. And he is unexcelled in taking apart structurally the Beethoven, Brahms, Tchaikovsky and other quartets, in analyzing and explaining the wonderful planning and building up of each movement. I had the honor of playing second violin in the Kneisel Quartet from September to February (1914–1915), at the outbreak of the war, a most interesting experience. The musicianship Kneisel had given me; I was used to his style and at home with his ideas, and am happy to think that he was satisfied. A year later as assistant concertmaster in the Chicago Symphony Orchestra, I had a chance to become practically acquainted with the orchestral works of Strauss, d'Indy and other moderns, and enjoy the Beethoven, Brahms and Tchaikovsky symphonies as a performer.

TECHNIQUE AND MUSICIANSHIP

"How do I regard technique now? I think of it in the terms of the music itself. Music should dictate the technical means to be used. The composition and its phrases should determine bowing and the tone quality employed. One should not think of down-bows or up-bows. In the Brahms *Concerto* you can find many long phrases: they cannot be played with one bow; yet there must be no apparent change of bow. If the player does not know what the phrase means; how to interpret it, how will he be able to bow it correctly?

"And there are so many different *nuances*, especially in *legato*. It is as a rule produced by a slurred bow; yet it may also be produced by other bowings. To secure a good *legato* tone watch the singer. The singer can establish the perfect smoothness that *legato* calls for to perfection. To secure a like effect the violinist should convey the impression that there is no point, no frog, that the bow he uses is of indefinite length. And the violinist should never think: 'I must play this up-bow or down-bow.' Artists of the German school are more apt to begin a phrase with a down-bow; the French start playing a good deal at the point. Up or down, both are secondary to finding out, first of all, what quality, what balance of tone the phrase demands. The conductor of a symphonic orchestra does not care how, technically, certain effects are produced by the violins, whether they use an up-bow or a down-bow. He merely says: 'That's too heavy: give me less tone!' The result to be achieved is always more important than the manner of achievement.

"All phases of technical accomplishment, if rightly acquired, tend to become second nature to the player in the course of time: *staccato,* a brilliant trick; *spiccato,* the reiteration of notes played from the wrist, etc. The *martellato,* a *nuance* of *spiccato,* should be played with a firm bowing at the point. In a very broad *spiccato,* the arm may be brought into play; but otherwise not, since it makes rapid playing impossible. Too many amateurs try to play *spiccato* from the arm. And too many teachers are contented with a trill that is merely brilliant. Kneisel insists on what he calls a 'musical trill,' of which Kreisler's beautiful trill is a perfect example. The trill of some violinists is *invariably* brilliant, whether brilliancy is appropriate or not. Brilliant trills in Bach always seem out of place to me; while in Paganini and in Wieniawski's *Carnaval de Venise* a high brilliant trill is very effective.

"As to double-stops—Edison once said that violin music should be written only in double-stops—I practice them playing first the single notes and then the two together, and can recommend this mode of practice from personal experience. Harmonics, where clarity is the most important thing, are mainly a matter of bowing, of a sure attack and sustaining by the bow. Of course the harmonics themselves are made by the fingers; but their tone quality rests altogether with the bow.

EDISON AND OCTAVES

"The best thing I've ever heard said of octaves was Edison's remark to me that 'They are merely a nuisance and should not be played!' I was making some records for him during the experimental stage of the disk record, when he was trying to get an absolutely smooth *legato* tone, one that conformed to Loeffler's definition of it as 'no breaks' in the tone. He had had Schubert's *Ave Maria* recorded by Flesch, MacMillan and others, and wanted me to play it for him. The records were all played for me, and whenever he came to the octave passages Edison would say: 'Listen to them! How badly they sound!' Yet the octaves were absolutely in tune! 'Why do they sound so badly?' I inquired.

"Then Edison explained to me that according to the scientific theory of vibration, the vibrations of the higher tone of the octaves should be exactly twice those of the lower note. 'But here,' he continued, 'the vibrations of the notes all vary.' 'Yet how can the player control his fingers in the *vibrato* beyond playing his octaves in perfect tune?' I asked. 'Well, if he cannot do so,' said Edison, 'octaves are merely a nuisance, and should not be played at all.' I experimented and found that by simply pressing down the fingers and playing without any *vibrato*, I could come pretty near securing the exact relation between the vibrations of the upper and lower notes but—they sounded dreadful! Of course, octaves sound well in *ensemble*, especially in the orchestra, because each player plays but a single note. And tenths sound even better than octaves when two people play them.

WIRE AND GUT STRINGS

"You ask about my violin? It belonged to the famous Hawley collection, and is a Giovanni Baptista Guadignini, made in 1780, in Turin. The back is a single piece of maple-wood, having a broadish figure extending across its breadth. The maple-wood sides match the back. The top is formed of a very choice piece of spruce, and it is varnished a deep golden-red. It has a remarkably fine tone, very vibrant and with great carrying power, a tone that has all that I can ask for as regards volume and quality.

"I think that wire strings are largely used now-a-days because gut strings are hard to obtain—not because they are better. I do not use wire strings. I have tried them and find them thin in tone, or so brilliant that their tone is too piercing. Then, too, I find that the use of a wire E reduces the volume of tone of the

other strings. No wire string has the quality of a fine gut string;
and I regard them only as a substitute in the case of some people, and a convenience for lazy ones.

VIOLIN MASTERY

"'Violin Mastery'? Off-hand I might say the phrase stands for
a life-time of effort with its highest aims unattained. As I see it
the achievement of 'Violin Mastery' represents a combination of
90 percent of toil and 10 percent of talent or inspiration.
Goetschius, with whom I studied composition, once said to me:
'I do not congratulate you on having talent. That is a gift. But I
do congratulate you on being able to work hard!' The same thing
applies to the fiddle. It seems to me that only by keeping ever-
lastingly at it can one become a master of the instrument."

ARTHUR HARTMANN

THE PROBLEM OF TECHNIQUE

A rthur Hartmann is distinctly and unmistakably a personality. He stands out even in that circle of distinguished contemporary violinists which is so largely made up of personalities.
He is a composer—not only of violin pieces, but of symphonic
and choral works, chamber music, songs and piano numbers.
His critical analysis of Bach's *Chaconne,* translated into well-
nigh every tongue, is probably the most complete and exhaustive study of "that triumph of genius over matter" written. And
besides being a master of his own instrument he plays the *viola
d'amore,* that sweet-toned survival, with sympathetic strings, of
the 17th century viol family, and the Hungarian *czimbalom.* Nor
is his mastery of the last-named instrument "out of drawing," for
we must remember that Mr. Hartmann was born in Maté
Szalka, in Southern Hungary. Then, too, Mr. Hartmann is a
genial and original thinker, a *littérateur* of no mean ability, a bib-
liophile, the intimate of the late Claude Debussy, and of many
of the great men of musical Europe. Yet from the reader's standpoint the interest he inspires is, no doubt, mainly due to the fact
that not only is he a great interpreting artist—but a great artist
doubled by a great teacher, an unusual combination.

Characteristic of Mr. Hartmann's hospitality (the writer had
passed a pleasant hour with him some years before, but had not
seen him since), was the fact that he insisted in brewing Turkish
coffee, and making his caller feel quite at home before even
allowing him to broach the subject of his visit. And when he
learned that its purpose was to draw on his knowledge and expe-

ARTHUR HARTMANN

rience for information which would be of value to the serious student and lover of his art, he did not refuse to respond.

WHAT VIOLIN PLAYING REALLY IS

"Violin playing is really no abstract mystery. It's as clear as geography in a way: one might say the whole art is bounded on the South by the G string, on the North by the E string, on the West by the string hand—and that's about as far as the comparison may be carried out. The point is, there are definite boundaries, whose technical and æsthetic limits may be extended, and territorial annexations made through brain power, mental control. To me 'Violin Mastery' means taking this little fiddle-box in hand [and Mr. Hartmann suited action to word by raising the lid of his violin-case and drawing forth his beautiful 1711 Strad], and doing just what I want with it. And that means having the right finger on the right place at the right time—but don't forget that to be able to do this you must have forgotten to think of your fingers as fingers. They should be simply unconscious slaves of the artist's psychic expression, absolutely subservient to his ideal. Too many people reverse the process and become slaves to their fingers.

THE PROBLEM OF TECHNIQUE

"Technique, for instance, in its mechanical sense, is a much exaggerated microbe of *Materia musica.* All technique must conform to its instrument.* The violin was made to suit the hand, not the hand to suit the violin, hence its technique must be based on a natural logic of hand movement. The whole problem of technical control is encountered in the first change of position on the violin. If we violinists could play in but one position there would be no technical problem. The solution of this problem means, speaking broadly, the ability to play the violin— for there is only one way of playing it—with a real, full, singing 'violin' tone. It's not a question of a method, but just a process based on pure reason, the working out of rational principles.

---

*This is the idea which underlies my system for ear-training and absolute pitch, "Arthur Hartmann's System," as I call it, which I have published. A. H.

"What is the secret of this singing tone? Well, you may call it a secret, for many of my pupils have no inkling of it when they first come here, though it seems very much of an 'open secret' to me. The finished beauty of the violin 'voice' is a round, sustained, absolutely smooth *cantabile* tone. Now [Mr. Hartmann took up his Strad], I'll play you the scale of G as the average violin student plays it. You see—each slide from one tone to the next, a break—a rosary of lurches! How can there be a round, harmonious tone when the fingers progress by jerks? Shifting position must not be a continuous movement of effort, but a continuous movement in which effort and relaxation—that of dead weight—alternate. As an illustration, when we walk we do not consciously set down one foot, and then swing forward the other foot and leg with a jerk. The forward movement is smooth, unconscious, coordinated: in putting the foot forward it carries the weight of the entire body, the movement becomes a matter of instinct. And the same applies to the progression of the fingers in shifting the position of the hand. Now, playing the scale as I now do—only two fingers should be used—

I prepare every shift. Absolute accuracy of intonation and a singing *legato* is the result. These guiding notes indicated are merely a test to prove the scientific spacing of the violin; they are not sounded once control of the hand has been obtained. *They serve only to accustom the fingers to keep moving in the direction in which they are going.*

"The tone is produced by the left hand, by the weight of the fingers plus an undercurrent of sustained effort. Now, you see, *if in the moment of sliding you prepare the bow for the next string, the slide itself is lost in the crossing of the bow.* To carry out consistently this idea of effort and relaxation in the downward progression of the scale, you will find that when you are in the third position, the position of the hand is practically the same as in the first position. Hence, in order to go down from third to first position with the hand in what might be called a 'block' position, another movement is called for to bridge over this space (between third and first position), and this movement is the function of the thumb. The thumb, preceding the hand, relaxes the wrist and helps draw the hand back to first position. But great care must be taken that the thumb is not moved until the first finger will have been played; otherwise there will be a tendency to flatten. In the illustration the indication for the thumb is placed after the note played by the first finger.

"The inviolable law of beautiful playing is that there must be no angles. As I have shown you, right and left hand coordinate. The fiddle hand is preparing the change of position, while the change of strings is prepared by the right hand. And always the slides in the left hand are prepared by the last played finger— *the last played finger is the true guide to smooth progression*— just as the bow hand prepares the slides in the last played bowing. There should be no such thing as jumping and trusting in Providence to land right, and a curse ought to be laid on those who let their fingers leave the fingerboard. None who develop this fundamental aspect of all good playing lose the perfect control of position.

"Of course there are a hundred *nuances* of technique (into which the quality of good taste enters largely) that one could talk of at length: phrasing, and the subtle things happening in the bow arm that influence it; *spiccato,* whose whole secret is finding the right point of balance in the bow and, with light finger control, never allowing it to leave the string. I've never been able to see the virtue of octaves or the logic of double-stops. Like tenths, one plays or does not play them. But do they add one iota of beauty to violin music? I doubt it! And, after all, it is the poetry of playing that counts. All violin playing in its essence is the quest for color; its perfection, that subtle art which hides art, and which is so rarely understood."

"Could you give me a few guiding rules, a few Beatitudes, as it were, for the serious student to follow?" I asked Mr.

Hartmann. Though the artist smiled at the idea of Beatitudes for the violinist, yet he was finally amiable enough to give me the following, telling me I would have to take them for what they were worth:

NINE BEATITUDES FOR VIOLINISTS

"Blessed are they who early in life approach Bach, for their love and veneration for music will multiply with the years.

"Blessed are they who remember their own early struggles, for their merciful criticism will help others to a greater achievement and furtherance of the Divine Art.

"Blessed are they who know their own limitations, for they shall have joy in the accomplishment of others.

"Blessed are they who revere the teachers—their own or those of others—and who remember them with credit.

"Blessed are they who, revering the old masters, seek out the newer ones and do not begrudge them a hearing or two.

"Blessed are they who work in obscurity, nor sound the trumpet, for Art has ever been for the few, and shuns the vulgar blare of ignorance.

"Blessed are they whom men revile as futurists and modernists, for Art can evolve only through the medium of iconoclastic spirits.

"Blessed are they who unflinchingly serve their Art, for thus only is their happiness to be gained.

"Blessed are they who have many enemies, for square pegs will never fit into round holes."

ARRANGING VERSUS TRANSCRIBING

Arthur Hartmann, like Kreisler, Elman, Maud Powell and others of his colleagues, has enriched the literature of the violin with some notably fine transcriptions. And it is a subject on which he has well-defined opinions and regarding which he makes certain distinctions: "An 'arrangement,'" he said, "as a rule, is a purely commercial affair, into which neither art nor æsthetics enter. It usually consists in writing off the melody of a song—in other words, playing the 'tune' on an instrument instead of hearing it sung with words—or in the case of a piano composition, in writing off the upper voice, leaving the rest intact, regardless of sonority, tone-color or even effectiveness, and, furthermore, without consideration of the idiomatic principles of the instrument to which the adaptation was meant to fit.

"A 'transcription,' on the other hand, can be raised to the dignity of an art-work. Indeed, at times it may even surpass the original, in the quality of thought brought into the work, the delicate and sympathetic treatment and by the many subleties which an artist can introduce to make it thoroughly a *re-creation* of his chosen instrument.

"It is the transcriber's privilege—providing he be sufficiently the artist to approach the personality of another artist with reverence—to donate his own gifts of ingenuity, and to exercise his judgment in either adding, omitting, harmonically or otherwise embellishing the work (*while preserving the original idea and characteristics*), so as to thoroughly *re-create* it, so completely destroying the very sensing of the original *timbre* that one involuntarily exclaims, 'Truly, this never was anything but a violin piece!' It is this, the blending and fusion of two personalities in the achievement of an art-ideal, that is the result of a true adaptation.

"Among the transcriptions I have most enjoyed making were those of Debussy's *Il pleure dans mon cœur,* and *La Fille aux cheveaux de lin.* Debussy was my cherished friend, and they represent a labor of love. Though Debussy was not, generally speaking, an advocate of transcriptions, he liked these, and I remember when I first played *La Fille aux cheveaux de lin* for him, and came to a bit of counterpoint I had introduced in the violin melody, whistling the harmonics, he nodded approvingly with a *'pas bête ça!'* (Not stupid, that!)

DEBUSSY'S POÈME FOR VIOLIN

"Debussy came near writing a violin piece for me once!" continued Mr. Hartmann, and brought out a folio containing letters the great impressionist had written him. They were a delightful revelation of the human side of Debussy's character, and Mr. Hartmann kindly consented to the quotation of one bearing on the *Poème* for violin which Debussy had promised to write for him, and which, alas, owing to his illness and other reasons, never actually came to be written:

"Dear Friend:

"Of course I am working a great deal now, because I feel the need of writing music, and would find it difficult to build an aeroplane; yet at times Music is ill-natured, even toward those who love her most! Then I take my little daughter and my hat and go walking in the Bois de Boulogne, where one meets people who have come from afar to bore themselves in Paris.

"I think of you, I might even say I am in need of you (assume an air of exaltation and bow, if you please!) As to the *Poème* for violin, you may rest assured that I will write it. Only at the present moment I am so preoccupied with the 'Fall of the House of Usher!' They talk too much to me about it. I'll have to put an end to all that or I will go mad. Once more I want to write it, and above all *on your account.* And I believe you will be the only one to play the *Poème.* Others will attempt it, and then quickly return to the Mendelssohn *Concerto!*

"Believe me always your sincere friend,

"CLAUDE DEBUSSY."

"He never did write it," said Mr. Hartmann, "but it was not for want of good will. As to other transcriptions, I have never done any that I did not feel instinctively would make good fiddle pieces, such as MacDowell's *To a Wild Rose* and others of his compositions. And recently I have transcribed some fine Russian things—Gretchaninoff's *Chant d'Automne,* Karagitscheff's *Exaltation,* Tchaikovsky's *Humoresque,* Balakirev's *Chant du Pechêur,* and Poldini's little *Poupée valsante,* which Maud Powell plays so delightfully on all her programs."

JASCHA HEIFETZ

THE DANGER OF PRACTICING TOO MUCH.
TECHNICAL MASTERY AND TEMPERAMENT

Mature in virtuosity—the modern virtuosity which goes so far beyond the mere technical mastery that once made the term a reproach—though young in years, Jascha Heifetz, when one makes his acquaintance "off-stage," seems singularly modest about the great gifts which have brought him international fame. He is amiable, unassuming and—the best proof, perhaps, that his talent is a thing genuine and inborn, not the result of a forcing process—he has that broad interest in art and in life going far beyond his own particular medium, the violin, without which no artist may become truly great. For Jascha Heifetz, with his wonderful record of accomplishment achieved, and with triumphs still to come before him, does not believe in "all work and no play."

THE DANGER OF PRACTICING TOO MUCH

He laughed when I put forward the theory that he worked many hours a day, perhaps as many as six or eight? "No," he said, "I do not think I could ever have made any progress if I had practiced six hours a day. In the first place I have never believed in practicing too much—it is just as bad as practicing too little! And then there are so many other things I like to do. I am fond of reading and I like sport: tennis, golf, bicycle riding, boating, swimming, etc. Often when I am supposed to be practicing hard I am out with my camera, taking pictures; for I have become what is known as a 'camera fiend.' And just now I have a new

JASCHA HEIFETZ

car, which I have learned to drive, and which takes up a good deal of my time. I have never believed in grinding. In fact I think that if one has to work very hard to get his piece, it will show in the execution. To interpret music properly, it is necessary to eliminate mechanical difficulty; the audience should not feel the struggle of the artist with what are considered hard passages. I hardly ever practice more than three hours a day on an average, and besides, I keep my Sunday when I do not play at all, and sometimes I make an extra holiday. As to six or seven hours a day, I would not have been able to stand it at all."

I implied that what Mr. Heifetz said might shock thousands of aspiring young violinists for whom he pointed a moral: "Of course," his answer was, "you must not take me too literally. Please do not think because I do not favor overdoing practicing that one can do without it. I'm quite frank to say I could not myself. But there is a happy medium. I suppose that when I play in public it looks easy, but before I ever came on the concert stage I worked very hard. And I do yet—but always putting the two things together, mental work and physical work. And when a certain point of effort is reached in practice, as in everything else, there must be relaxation.

THE DEVELOPMENT OF A VIRTUOSE TECHNIQUE

"Have I what is called a 'natural' technique? It is hard for me to say, perhaps so. But if such is the case I had to develop it, to assure it, to perfect it. If you start playing at three, as I did, with a little violin one-quarter of the regular size, I suppose violin playing becomes second nature in the course of time. I was able to find my way about in all seven positions within a year's time, and could play the Kayser *études;* but that does not mean to say I was a virtuoso by any means.

"My first teacher? My first teacher was my father, a good violinist and concertmaster of the Vilna Symphony Orchestra. My first appearance in public took place in an overcrowded auditorium of the Imperial Music School in Vilna, Russia, when I was not quite five. I played the *Fantaisie Pastorale* with piano accompaniment. Later, at the age of six, I played the Mendelssohn *Concerto* in Kovno to a full house. Stage-fright? No, I cannot say I have ever had it. Of course, something may happen to upset one before a concert, and one does not feel quite at ease when first stepping on the stage; but then I hope that is not stage-fright!

"At the Imperial Music School in Vilna, and before, I worked at all the things every violinist studies—I think that I played almost everything. I did not work too hard, but I worked hard enough. In Vilna my teacher was Malkin, a pupil of Professor Auer, and when I had graduated from the Vilna school I went to Auer. Did I go directly to his classes? Well, no, but I had only a very short time to wait before I joined the classes conducted by Auer personally.

PROFESSOR AUER AS A TEACHER

"Yes, he is a wonderful and an incomparable teacher; I do not believe there is one in the world who can possibly approach him. Do not ask me just how he does it, for I would not know how to tell you. But he is different with each pupil—perhaps that is one reason he is so great a teacher. I think I was with Professor Auer about six years, and I had both class lessons and private lessons of him, though toward the end my lessons were not so regular. I never played exercises or technical works of any kind for the Professor, but outside of the big things—the concertos and sonatas, and the shorter pieces which he would let me prepare—I often chose what I wanted.

"Professor Auer was a very active and energetic teacher. He was never satisfied with a mere explanation, unless certain it was understood. He could always show you himself with his bow and violin. The Professor's pupils were supposed to have been sufficiently advanced in the technique necessary for them to profit by his wonderful lessons in interpretation. Yet there were all sorts of technical *finesses* which he had up his sleeve, any number of fine, subtle points in playing as well as interpretation which he would disclose to his pupils. And the more interest and ability the pupil showed, the more the Professor gave him of himself! He is a very great teacher! Bowing, the true art of bowing, is one of the greatest things in Professor Auer's teaching. I know when I first came to the Professor, he showed me things in bowing I had never learned in Vilna. It is hard to describe in words [Mr. Heifetz illustrated with some of those natural, unstrained movements of arm and wrist which his concert appearances have made so familiar], but bowing as Professor Auer teaches it is a very special thing; the movements of the bow become more easy, graceful, less stiff.

"In class there were usually from twenty-five to thirty pupils. Aside from what we each gained individually from the Professor's criticism and correction, it was interesting to hear the others who played before one's turn came, because one could get all kinds of hints from what Professor Auer told them. I know I always enjoyed listening to Poliakin, a very talented violinist, and Cécile Hansen, who attended the classes at the same time I did. The Professor was a stern and very exacting, but a sympathetic, teacher. If our playing was not just what it should be he always had a fund of kindly humor upon which to draw. He would anticipate our stock excuses and say: 'Well, I suppose you have just had your bow rehaired!' or 'These new strings are very trying,' or 'It's the weather that is against you again, is it not?' or something of the kind. Examinations were not so easy: we had to show that we were not only soloists, but also sight readers of difficult music.

A DIFFICULTY OVERCOME

"The greatest technical difficulty I had when I was studying?" Jascha Heifetz tried to recollect, which was natural, seeing that it must have been one long since overcome. Then he remembered, and smiled: "*Staccato* playing. To get a good *staccato,* when I first tried seemed very hard to me. When I was younger, really, at one time I had a very poor *staccato!*" [I assured the young artist that any one who heard him play here would find it hard to believe this.] "Yes, I did," he insisted, "but one morning, I do not know just how it was—I was playing the *cadenza* in the first movement of Wieniawski's *F sharp minor concerto,*—it is full of *staccatos* and double-stops—the right way of playing *staccato* came to me quite suddenly, especially after Professor Auer had shown me his method.

VIOLIN MASTERY

" 'Violin Mastery'? To me it means the ability to make the violin a perfectly controlled instrument guided by the skill and intelligence of the artist, to compel it to respond in movement to his every wish. The artist must always be superior to his instrument, it must be his servant, one that he can do with what he will.

TECHNICAL MASTERY AND TEMPERAMENT

"It appears to me that mastery of the technique of the violin is not so much of a mechanical accomplishment as it is of mental nature. It may be that scientists can tell us how through persistency the brain succeeds in making the fingers and the arms produce results through the infinite variety of inexplicable vibrations. The sweetness of tone, its melodiousness, its *legatos*, octaves, trills and harmonics all bear the mark of the individual who uses his strings like his vocal chords. When an artist is working over his harmonics, he must not be impatient and force purity, pitch, or the right intonation. He must coax the tone, try it again and again, seek for improvements in his fingering as well as in his bowing at the same time, and sometimes he may be surprised how, quite suddenly, at the time when he least expects it, the result has come. More than one road leads to Rome! The fact is that when you get it, you have it, that's all! I am perfectly willing to disclose to the musical profession all the secrets of the mastery of violin technique; but are there any secrets in the sense that some of the uninitiated take them? If an artist happens to excel in some particular, he is at once suspected of knowing some secret means of so doing. However, that may not be the case. He does it just because it is in him, and as a rule he accomplishes this through his mental faculties more than through his mechanical abilities. I do not intend to minimize the value of great teachers who prove to be important factors in the life of a musician; but think of the vast army of pupils that a master teacher brings forth, and listen to the infinite variety of their *spiccatos*, octaves, *legatos*, and trills! For the successful mastery of violin technique let each artist study carefully his own individuality, let him concentrate his mental energy on the quality of pitch he intends to produce, and sooner or later he will find his way of expressing himself. Music is not only in the fingers or in the elbow. It is in that mysterious EGO of the man, it is his soul; and his body is like his violin, nothing but a tool. Of course, the great master must have the tools that suit him best, and it is the happy combination that makes for success.

"By the vibrations and modulations of the notes one may recognize the violinist as easily as we recognize the singer by his voice. Who can explain how the artist harmonizes the trilling of his fingers with the emotions of his soul?

"An artist will never become great through mere imitation, and never will he be able to attain the best results only by methods adopted by others. He must have his own initiative, although he will surely profit by the experience of others. Of course there are standard ways of approaching the study of violin technique; but these are too well known to dwell upon them: as to the niceties of the art, they must come from within. You can make a musician but not an artist!

REPERTORY AND PROGRAMS

"Which of the master works do I like best? Well, that is rather hard to answer. Each master work has its own beauties. Naturally one likes best what one understands best. I prefer to play the classics like Brahms, Beethoven, Mozart, Bach, Mendelssohn, etc. However, I played Bruch's *G minor* in 1913 at the Leipzig Gewandhouse with Nikisch, where I was told that Joachim was the only other violinist as young as myself to appear there as soloist with orchestra; there is the Tchaikovsky *Concerto* which I played in Berlin in 1912, with the Berlin Philharmonic Orchestra with Nikisch. Alsa Bruch's *D minor* and many more. I played the Mendelssohn *Concerto* in 1914, in Vienna, with Safonoff as conductor. Last season in Chicago I played the Brahms concerto with a fine and very elaborate *cadenza* by Professor Auer. I think the Brahms *Concerto* for violin is like Chopin's music for piano, in a way, because it stands technically and musically for something quite different and distinct from other violin music, just as Chopin does from other piano music. The Brahms concerto is not technically as hard as, say, Paganini—but in interpretation! . . . And in the Beethoven *Concerto,* too, there is a simplicity, a kind of clear beauty which makes it far harder to play than many other things technically more advanced. The slightest flaw, the least difference in pitch, in intonation, and its beauty suffers.

"Yes, there are other Russian concertos besides the Tchaikovsky. There is the Glazunov *Concerto* and others. I understand that Zimbalist was the first to introduce it in this country, and I expect to play it here next season.

"Of course one cannot always play concertos, and one cannot always play Bach and Beethoven. And that makes it hard to select programs. The artist can always enjoy the great music of his instrument; but an audience wants variety. At the same time an artist cannot play only just what the majority of the audience wants. I have been asked to play Schubert's *Ave Maria,* or Beethoven's *Chorus of Dervishes* at every one of my concerts, but I simply cannot play them all the time. I am afraid if program making were left altogether to audiences the programs would become far too popular in character; though audiences are just as different as individuals. I try hard to balance my programs, so that every one can find something to understand and enjoy. I expect to prepare some American compositions for next season. Oh, no, not as a matter of courtesy, but because they are really fine, especially some smaller pieces by Spalding, Cecil Burleigh and Grasse!"

On concluding our interview Mr. Heifetz made a remark which is worth repeating, and which many a music lover who is *plus royaliste que le roi* might do well to remember: "After all," he said, "much as I love music, I cannot help feeling that music is not the only thing in life. I really cannot imagine anything more terrible than always to hear, think and make music! There is so much else to know and appreciate; and I feel that the more I learn and know of other things the better artist I will be!"

DAVID HOCHSTEIN

THE VIOLIN AS A MEANS OF EXPRESSION
AND EXPRESSIVE PLAYING

The writer talked with Lieutenant David Hochstein, whose
death in the battle of the Argonne Forest was only reported
toward the end of January, while the distinguished young violinist, then only a sergeant, was on the eve of departure to France
with his regiment and, as he modestly said, his "thoughts on
music were rather scattered." Yet he spoke with keen insight
and authority on various phases of his art, and much of what he
said gains point from his own splendid work as a concert violinist; for Lieutenant Hochstein (whose standing has been established in numerous European as well as American recitals)
could play what he preached.

SEVČIK AND AUER: A CONTRAST IN TEACHING

Knowing that in the regimental band he was, quite appropri-
ately, a clarinetist, "the clarinet in the military band being the
equivalent of the violin in the orchestra"—and a scholarship
pupil of the Vienna *Meisterschule,* it seemed natural to ask him
concerning his teachers. And the interesting fact developed
that he had studied with the celebrated Bohemian pedagogue
Sevčik and with Leopold Auer as well, two teachers whose
ideas and methods differ materially. "I studied with Sevčik for
two years," said the young violinist. "It was in 1909, when a
class of ten pupils was formed for him in the *Meisterschule,* at
Vienna, that I went to him. Sevčik was in many ways a wonderful teacher, yet inclined to overemphasize the mechanical side

of the art. He literally *taught* his pupils how to practice, how to develop technical control by the most slow and painstaking study. In addition to his own fine method and exercises, he also used Gavinies, Dont, Rode, Kreutzer, applying in their studies ideas of his own.

"Auer as a teacher I found altogether different. Where Sevčik taught his pupils the technique of their art by means of a system elaborately worked out, Auer demonstrated his ideas through sheer personality, mainly from the interpretative point of view. Any ambitious student could learn much of value from either; yet in a general way one might express the difference between them by saying that Sevčik could take a pupil of medium talent and—at least from the mechanical stand-point—make an excellent violinist of him. But Auer is an ideal teacher for the greatly gifted. And he is especially skilled in taking some student of the violin while his mind is still plastic and susceptible and molding it—supplying it with lofty concepts of interpretation and expression. Of course Auer (I studied with him in Petrograd and Dresden) has been especially fortunate as regards his pupils, too, because active in a land like Russia, where musical genius has almost become a commonplace.

"Sevčik, though an admirable teacher, personally is of a reserved and reflective type, quite different from Auer, who is open and expansive. I might recall a little instance which shows Sevčik's cautious nature, the care he takes not to commit himself too unreservedly. When I took leave of him—it was after I had graduated and won my prize—I naturally (like all his pupils) asked him for his photo. Several other pupils of his were in the room at the time. He took up his pen (I was looking over his shoulder), commenced to write *Meinem best.* . . . And then he stopped, glanced at the other pupils in the room, and wrote over the *best* . . . he had already written, the word *liebsten.* But though I would, of course, have preferred the first inscription, had Sevčik completed it, I can still console myself that the other, even though I value it, was an afterthought. But it was a characteristic thing for him to do!

THE VIOLIN AS A MEANS OF EXPRESSION

"What is my idea of the violin as a medium of expression? It seems to me that it is that of any other valid artistic medium. It is not so much a question of the violin as of the violinist. A great interpreter reveals his inner-most soul through his instrument, whatever it may be. Most people think the violin is more expressive than any other instrument, but this is open to question. It may be that most people respond more readily to the appeal made by the violin. But genuine expression, expressive playing, depends on the message the player has to deliver far more than on the instrument he uses as a means. I have been as much moved by some piano playing I have heard as by the violin playing of some of the greatest violinists.

"And variety, *nuance* in expressive playing, is largely a matter of the player's mental attitude. Bach's *Chaconne* or *Sicilienne* calls for a certain humility on the part of the artist. When I play Bach I do it reverentially; a definite spiritual quality in my tone and expression is the result. And to select a composer who in many ways is Bach's exact opposite, Wieniawski, a certain audacious brilliancy cannot help but make itself felt tonally, if this music is to be played in character. The mental and spiritual attitude directly influences its own mechanical transmission. No one artist should criticize another for differences in interpretation, in expression, so long as they are justified by larger concepts of art. Individuality is one of the artist's most precious possessions, and there are always a number of different angles from which the interpretation of an art work may be approached.

VIOLIN MASTERY

"'Violin Mastery'? There have been only three violinists within my own recollection, whom I would call masters of the violin. These are Kubelik (when at his best), Franz von Vecsey, Hubay's pupil, whom I heard abroad, and Heifetz, with his cameo-like perfection of technique. These I would call masters of the violin, as an instrument, since they have mastered every intricacy of the instrument. But I could name several others who are greater musicians, and whose playing and interpretation, to say nothing of tone, I prefer.

TONE PRODUCTION: RHYTHM

"In one sense true violin mastery is a question of tone production and rhythm. And I believe that tone production depends principally upon the imaginative ear of the player. This statement may seem somewhat ambiguous, and one might ask, 'What is an imaginative ear?' My ear, for instance, demands of my violin a certain quality of tone, which varies according to the music I am playing. But before I think of playing the music, I already know from reading it what I want it to sound like: that is to say, the quality of the tone I wish to secure in each principal phrase. Rhythm is perhaps the greatest factor in interpretation. Every good musician has a 'good sense of rhythm' (that much abused phrase). But it is only the *great* musician who makes so striking and individual an application of rhythm that his playing may be easily distinguished by his use of it.

"There is not much to tell you as regards my method of work. I usually work directly upon a program which has been previously mapped out. If I have been away from my violin for more than a week or two I begin by practicing scales, but ordinarily I find my technical work in the programs I am preparing."

Asked about his band experiences at Camp Upton, Sergeant Hochstein was enthusiastic. "No violinist could help but gain much from work with a military band at one of the camps," he said. "For instance, I had a more or less theoretical knowledge of wind instruments before I went to Camp Upton. Now I have a practical working knowledge of them. I have already scored a little violin composition of mine, a *Minuet in Olden Style* for full band, and have found it possible by the right manipulation to preserve its original dainty and graceful character, in spite of the fact that it is played by more than forty military bandsmen.

"Then, too," he said in conclusion, "I have organized a real orchestra of twenty-one players, strings, brass, wood-wind, etc., which I hope is going to be of real use on the other side during our training period in France. You see, 'over there' the soldier boys' chances for leave are limited and we will have to depend a good deal on our own selves for amusement and recreation. I hope and believe my orchestra is not only going to take its place as one of the most enjoyable features of our army life; but also that it will make propaganda of the right sort for the best music in a broad, catholic sense of the word!"

It is interesting to know that this patriotic young officer found opportunities in camp and in the towns of France of carrying out his wish to "make propaganda of the right sort for the best music" before he gave his life to further the greater purpose which had called him overseas.

FRITZ KREISLER

PERSONALITY IN ART

The influence of the artist's personality in his art finds a most striking exemplification in the case of Fritz Kreisler. Some time before the writer called on the famous violinist to get at first hand some of his opinions with regard to his art, he had already met him under particularly interesting circumstances. The question had come up of writing text-poems for two song-adaptations of Viennese folk-themes, airs not unattractive in themselves; but which Kreisler's personal touch, his individual gift of harmonization had lifted from a lower plane to the level of the art song. Together with the mss. of his own beautiful transcript, Mr. Kreisler in the one instance had given me the printed original which suggested it—frankly a "popular" song, clumsily harmonized in a "four-square" manner (though written in 3/4 time) with nothing to indicate its latent possibilities. I compared it with his mss. and, lo, it had been transformed! Gone was the clumsiness, the vulgar and obvious harmonic treatment of the melody—Kreisler had kept the melodic outline, but etherealized, spiritualized it, given it new rhythmic *contours*, a deeper and more expressive meaning. And his rich and subtle harmonization had lent it a quality of distinction that justified a comparison between the grub and the butterfly. In a small way it was an illuminating glimpse of how the personality of a true artist can metamorphose what at first glance might seem something quite negligible, and create beauty where its possibilities alone had existed before.

It is this personal, this individual, note in all that Fritz Kreisler does—when he plays, when he composes, when he

FRITZ KREISLER

transcribes—that gives his art-effort so great and unique a quality of appeal.

Talking to him in his comfortable sitting-room in the Hotel
Wellington—Homer and Juvenal (in the original) ranked on the
piano-top beside De Vere Stackpole novels and other contemporary literature called to mind that though Brahms and
Beethoven violin concertos are among his favorites, he does not
disdain to play a Granados *Spanish Dance*—it seemed natural to
ask him how he came to make those adaptations and transcripts
which have been so notable a feature of his programs, and which
have given such pleasure to thousands.

HOW KREISLER CAME TO COMPOSE AND ARRANGE

He said: "I began to compose and arrange as a young man. I
wanted to create a repertory for myself, to be able to express
through my medium, the violin, a great deal of beautiful music
that had first to be adapted for the instrument. What I composed and arranged was for my own use, reflected my own
musical tastes and preferences. In fact, it was not till years after
that I even thought of publishing the pieces I had composed and
arranged. For I was very diffident as to the outcome of such a
step. I have never written anything with the commercial idea of
making it 'playable.' And I have always felt that anything done
in a cold-blooded way for purely mercenary considerations
somehow cannot be good. It cannot represent an artist's best."

AT THE VIENNA CONSERVATORY

In reply to another query Mr. Kreisler reverted to the days
when as a boy he studied at the Vienna Conservatory. "I was
only seven when I attended the Conservatory and was much
more interested in playing in the park, where my boy friends
would be waiting for me, than in taking lessons on the violin.
And yet some of the most lasting musical impressions of my life
were gathered there. Not so much as regards study itself, as with
respect to the good music I heard. Some very great men played
at the Conservatory when I was a pupil. There were Joachim,
Sarasate in his prime, Hellmesberger, and Rubinstein, whom I
heard play the first time he came to Vienna. I really believe that

hearing Joachim and Rubinstein play was a greater event in my life and did more for me than five years of study!"

"Of course you do not regard technique as the main essential of the concert violinist's equipment?" I asked him. "Decidedly not. Sincerity and personality are the first main essentials. Technical equipment is something which should be taken for granted. The *virtuoso* of the type of Ole Bull, let us say, has disappeared. The 'stunt' player of a former day with a repertory of three or four bravura pieces was not far above the average music-hall 'artist.' The modern *virtuoso*, the true concert artist, is not worthy of the title unless his art is the outcome of a completely unified nature.

VIOLIN MASTERY

"I do not believe that any artist is truly a master of his instrument unless his control of it is an integral part of a whole. The musician is born—his medium of expression is often a matter of accident. I believe one may be intended for an artist prenatally; but whether violinist, 'cellist or pianist is partly a matter of circumstance. 'Violin Mastery,' to my mind, still falls short of perfection, in spite of the completest technical and musical equipment, if the artist thinks only of the instrument he plays. After all, it is just a single medium of expression. The true musician is an artist with a special instrument. And every real artist has the feeling for other forms and mediums of expression if he is truly a master of his own.

TECHNIQUE VERSUS IMAGINATION

"I think the technical element in the artist's education is often unduly stressed. Remember," added Mr. Kreisler, with a smile, "I am not a teacher, and this is a purely personal opinion I am giving you. But it seems to me that absolute sincerity of effort, actual impossibility *not* to react to a genuine musical impulse are of great importance. I firmly believe that if one is destined to become an artist the technical means find themselves. The necessity of expression will follow the line of least resistance. Too great a manual equipment often leads to an exaggeration of the technical and tempts the artist to stress it unduly.

"I have worked a great deal in my life, but have always found that too large an amount of purely technico-musical work fatigued me and reacted unfavorably on my imagination. As a rule I only practice enough to keep my fingers in trim; the nervous strain is such that doing more is out of the question. And for a concert-violinist when on tour, playing every day, the technical question is not absorbing. Far more important is it for him to keep himself mentally and physically fresh and in the right mood for his work. For myself I have to enjoy whatever I play or I cannot play it. And it has often done me more good to dip my finger-tips in hot water for a few seconds before stepping out on the platform than to spend a couple of hours practicing. But I should not wish the student to draw any deductions from what I say on this head. It is purely personal and has no general application.

"Technical exercises I use very moderately. I wish my imagination to be responsive, my interest fresh, and as a rule I have found that too much work along routine channels does not accord with the best development of my Art. I feel that technique should be in the player's head, it should be a mental picture, a sort of 'master record.' It should be a matter of will power to which the manual possibilities should be subjected. Technique to me is a mental and not a manual thing.

MENTAL TECHNIQUE: ITS DRAWBACK AND ITS ADVANTAGE

"The technique thus achieved, a technique whose controlling power is chiefly mental, is not perfect—I say so frankly—because it is more or less dependent on the state of the artist's nervous system. Yet it is the one and only kind of technique that can adequately and completely express the musician's every instinct, wish and emotion. Every other form of technique is stiff, unpliable, since it cannot entirely subordinate itself to the individuality of the artist."

PRACTICE HOURS FOR THE ADVANCED STUDENT

Mr. Kreisler gives no lessons and hence referred this question in the most amiable manner to his boyhood friend and fellow-student Felix Winternitz, the well-known Boston violin teacher, one of the faculty of the New England Conservatory of Music, who had come in while we were talking. Mr. Winternitz did not refuse an answer: "The serious student, in my opinion, should not practice less than four hours a day, nor need he practice more than five. Other teachers may demand more. Sevčik, I know, insists that his pupils practice eight and ten hours a day. To do so one must have the constitution of an ox, and the results are often not equal to those produced by four hours of concentrated work. As Mr. Kreisler intimated with regard to technique, practice calls for brain power. Concentration in itself is not enough. There is only one way to work and if the pupil can find it he can cover the labor of weeks in an hour."

And turning to me, Mr. Winternitz added: "You must not take Mr. Kreisler too seriously when he lays no stress on his own practicing. During the concert season he has his violin in hand for an hour or so nearly every day. He does not call it practicing, and you and I would consider it playing and great playing at that. But it is a genuine illustration of what I meant when I said that one who knew how could cover the work of weeks in an hour's time."

AN EXPLANATION BY MR. WINTERNITZ

I tried to draw from the famous violinist some hint as to the secret of the abiding popularity of his own compositions and transcripts but—as those who know him are aware—Kreisler has all the modesty of the truly great. He merely smiled and said: "Frankly, I don't know." But Mr. Winternitz' comment (when a phone call had taken Kreisler from the room for a moment) was, "It is the touch given by his accompaniments that adds so much: a harmonic treatment so rich in design and coloring, and so varied that melodies were never more beautifully set off." Mr. Kreisler, as he came in again, remarked: "I don't mind telling you that I enjoyed very much writing my *Tambourin Chinois.*° The idea for it came to me after a visit to

---

°It is interesting to note that Nikolai Sokoloff, conductor of the San Francisco Philharmonic, returning from a tour of the American and French army camps in France, some time ago, said: "My most popular number was Kreisler's *Tambourin Chinois.* Invariably I had to repeat that." A strong endorsement of the internationalism of Art by the actual fighter in the trenches.

the Chinese theater in San Francisco—not that the music there suggested any theme, but it gave me the impulse to write a free fantasy in the Chinese manner."

STYLE, INTERPRETATION AND THE ARTISTIC IDEAL

The question of style now came up. "I am not in favor of 'labeling' the concert artist, of calling him a 'lyric' or a 'dramatic' or some other kind of a player. If he is an artist in the real sense he controls all styles." Then, in answer to another question: "Nothing can express music but music itself. Tradition in interpretation does not mean a cut-and-dried set of rules handed down; it is, or should be, a matter of individual sentiment, of inner conviction. What makes one man an artist and keeps another an amateur is a God-given instinct for the artistically and musically right. It is not a thing to be explained, but to be felt. There is often only a narrow line of demarcation between the artistically right and wrong. Yet nearly every real artist will be found to agree as to when and when not that boundary has been overstepped. Sincerity and personality as well as disinterestedness, an expression of himself in his art that is absolutely honest, these, I believe, are ideals which every artist should cherish and try to realize. I believe, furthermore, that these ideals will come more and more into their own; that after the war there will be a great uplift, and that Art will realize to the full its value as a humanizing factor in life." And as is well known, no great artist of our day has done more toward the actual realization of these ideals he cherishes than Fritz Kreisler himself.

FRANZ KNEISEL

THE PERFECT STRING ENSEMBLE

Is there a lover of chamber music unfamiliar with Franz Kneisel's name? It may be doubted. After earlier European triumphs the gifted Romanian violinist came to this country (1885), and aside from his activities in other directions—as a solo artist he was the first to play the Brahms and Goldmark violin concertos, and the César Franck *Sonata* in this country—organized his famous quartet. And, until his recent retirement as its director and first violin, it has been perhaps the greatest single influence toward stimulating appreciation for the best in chamber music that the country has known. Before the Flonzaley was, the Kneisels were. They made plain how much of beauty the chamber music repertory offered the amateur string player; not only in the classic repertory—Haydn, Mozart, Beethoven, Spohr; in Schubert, Schumann, Brahms; but in Smetana, Dvořák and Tchaikovsky; in César Franck, Debussy and Ravel. Not the least among Kneisel's achievements is, that while the professional musicians in the cities in which his organization played attended its concerts as a matter of course, the average music lover who played a string instrument came to them as well, and carried away with him a message delivered with all the authority of superb musicianship and sincerity, one which bade him "go and do likewise," in so far as his limitations permitted. And the many excellent professional chamber music organizations, trios, quartets and *ensembles* of various kinds which have come to the fore since they began to play offer eloquent testimony with regard to the cultural work of Kneisel and his fellow artists.

FRANZ KNEISEL

A cheery grate fire burned in the comfortable study in Franz
Kneisel's home; the autographed—in what affectionate and
appreciative terms—pictures of great fellow artists looked down
above the bookcases which hold the scores of those masters of
what has been called "the noblest medium of music in existence," whose beauties the famous quartet has so often disclosed on the concert stage. And Mr. Kneisel was amiability
personified when I asked him to give me his theory of the perfect string *ensemble*, and the part virtuosity played in it.

"THE ARTIST RANKS THE VIRTUOSO
IN CHAMBER MUSIC"

"The artist, the *Tonkünstler*, to use a foreign phrase, ranks the
virtuoso in chamber music. Joachim was no virtuoso, he did not
stress technique, the less important factor in *ensemble* playing.
Sarasate was a virtuoso in the best sense of the word; and yet as
an *ensemble* music player he fell far short of Joachim. As I see it
'virtuoso' is a kind of flattering title, no more. But a *Tonkünstler*,
a 'tone-artist,' though he must have the virtuoso technique in
order to play Brahms and Beethoven *Concertos,* needs besides
a spiritual insight, a deep concept of their nobility to do them
justice—the mere technique demanded for a virtuoso show
piece is not enough.

VIOLIN MASTERY IN THE STRING QUARTET

"You ask me what 'Violin Mastery' means in the string quartet. It has an altogether different meaning to me, I imagine,
than to the violin virtuoso. 'Violin Mastery' in the string *ensemble* is as much mastery of self as of technical means. The artist
must sink his identity completely in that of the work he plays,
and though the last Beethoven quartets are as difficult as many
violin concertos, they are polyphony, the combination and interweaving of individual melodies, and they call for a mastery of
repression as well as expression. I realized how keenly alive the
musical listener is to this fact once when our quartet had played
in Alma-Tadema's beautiful London home, for the great English
painter was also a music lover and a very discriminating one. He
had a fine piano in a beautifully decorated case, and it was an

open secret that at his musical evenings, after an artist had
played, the lid of the piano was raised, and Sir Lawrence asked
him to pencil his autograph on the soft white wood of its inner
surface—*but only if he thought the compliment deserved.* There
were some famous names written there—Joachim, Sarasate,
Paderewski, Neruda, Piatti, to mention a few. Naturally an artist
playing at Alma-Tadema's home for the first time could not help
speculating as to his chances. Many were called, but comparatively few were chosen. We were guests at a dinner given by Sir
Lawrence. There were some fifty people prominent in London's
artistic, musical and social world present, and we had no idea of
being asked to play. Our instruments were at our hotel and we
had to send for them. We played the Schubert *Quartet in A
minor* and Dvořák's *American Quartet* and, of course, my colleagues and myself forgot all about the piano lid the moment we
began to play. Yet, I'm free to confess, that when the piano lid
was raised for us we appreciated it, for it was no empty compliment coming from Sir Lawrence, and I have been told that
some very distinguished artists have not had it extended to
them. And I know that on that evening the phrase 'Violin
Mastery' in an *ensemble* sense, as the outcome of ceaseless striving for coordination in expression, absolute balance, and all the
details that go to make up the perfect *ensemble,* seemed to us to
have a very definite color and meaning.

THE FIRST VIOLIN IN THE STRING QUARTET

"What exactly does the first violin represent?" Mr. Kneisel
went on in answer to another question. "The first violin might
be called the chairman of the string meeting. His is the leading
voice. Not that he should be an autocrat, no, but he must hold
the reins of discipline. Many think that the four string players in
a quartet have equal rights. First of all, and above all, are the
rights of the composer, Bach, Beethoven, Brahms, Schubert,—
as the case may be. But from the standpoint of interpretation
the first violin has some seventy percent of the responsibility as
compared with thirty percent for the remaining voices. In all
the famous quartet organizations, Joachim, Hellmesberger, etc.,
the first violin has been the directing instrument and has set the

pace. As chairman it has been his duty to say when second violin, viola and cello were entitled to hold the floor. Hellmesberger, in fact, considered himself the *whole* quartet." Mr. Kneisel
smiled and showed me a little book of Hellmesberger's Vienna
programs. Each program was headed:

HELLMESBERGER QUARTET

with the assistance of

MESSRS. MATH. DURST, CARL HEISSLER,
CARL SCHLESINGER

"In other words, Hellmesberger was the quartet himself, the
other three artists merely 'assisted,' which, after all, is going too
far!

"Of course, quartets differ. Just as we have operas in which
the alto solo *rôle* is the most important, so we have quartets in
which the cello or the viola has a more significant part. Mozart
dedicated quartets to a King of Prussia, who played cello, and he
was careful to make the cello part the most important. And in
Smetana's quartet *Aus meinem Leben*, the viola plays a most
important rôle. Even the second violin often plays themes intro-
ducing principal themes of the first violin, and it has its brief
moments of prominence. Yet, though the second violin or the
'cellist may be, comparatively speaking, a better player than the
first violin, the latter is and must be the leader. Practically every
composer of chamber music recognizes the fact in his compositions. He, the first violin, should not command three slaves,
though; but guide three associates, and do it tactfully with
regard to their individuality and that of their instruments.

"ENSEMBLE" REHEARSING

"You ask what are the essentials of *ensemble* practice on the
part of the artists? Real reverence, untiring zeal and punctuali-
ty at rehearsals. And then, an absolute sense of rhythm. I
remember rehearsing a Volkmann quartet once with a new second violinist." [Mr. Kneisel crossed over to his bookcase and
brought me the score to illustrate the rhythmic point in question, one slight in itself yet as difficult, perhaps, for a player

without an absolute sense of rhythm as "perfect intonation" would be for some others.] "He had a lovely tone, a big technique and was a prize pupil of the Vienna Conservatory. We went over this two measure phrase some sixteen times, until I felt sure he had grasped the proper accentuation. And he was most amiable and willing about it, too. But when we broke up he pointed to the passage and said to me with a smile: 'After all, whether you play it *this* way, or *that* way, what's the difference?' Then I realized that he had stressed his notes correctly a few times by chance, and that his own sense of rhythm did not tell him that there were no two ways about it. The rhythmic and tonal *nuances* in a quartet cannot be marked too perfectly in order to secure a beautiful and finished performance. And such a violinist as the one mentioned, in spite of his tone and technique, was never meant for an *ensemble* player.

"I have never believed in a quartet getting together and 'reading' a new work as a preparation for study. As first violin I have always made it my business to first study the work in score, myself, to study it until I knew the whole composition absolutely, until I had a mental picture of its meaning, and of the interrelation of its four voices in detail. Thirty-two years of experience have justified my theory. Once the first violin knows the work the practicing may begin; for he is in a position gradually and tactfully to guide the working-out of the interpretation without losing time in the struggle to correct faults in balance which are developed in an unprepared 'reading' of the work. There is always one important melody, and it is easier to find it studying the score, to trace it with eye and mind in its contrapuntal web, than by making voyages of discovery in actual playing.

"Every player has his own qualities, every instrument its own advantages. Certain passages in a second violin or viola part may be technically better suited to the hand of the player, to the nature of the instrument, and—they will sound better than others. Yet from the standpoint of the composition the passages that 'lie well' are often not the more important. This is hard for the player—what is easy for him he unconsciously is inclined to stress, and he must be on his guard against it.

This is another strong argument in favor of a thorough preliminary study on the part of the leading violin of the construction of the work."

THE FIRST VIOLIN IN CHAMBER MUSIC
VERSUS THE ORCHESTRA CONDUCTOR

The comparison which I asked Mr. Kneisel to make is one which he could establish with authority. Aside from his experience as director of his quartet, he has been the *concert-meister* of such famous foreign orchestras as Bilse's and that of the *Hofburg Theater* in Vienna and, for eighteen years, of the Boston Symphony Orchestra in this country. He has also conducted over one hundred concerts of the Boston Symphony, and was director of the Worcester Music Festivals.

"Nikisch once said to me, after he had heard us play the Schumann *A minor Quartet* in Boston: 'Kneisel, it was beautiful, and I felt that you had more difficulty in developing it than I have with an orchestral score!' And I think he was right. First of all the symphonic conductor is an autocrat. There is no appeal from the commands of his baton. But the first violin of a quartet is, in a sense, only the 'first among peers.' The velvet glove is an absolute necessity in his case. He must gain his art ends by diplomacy and tact, he must always remember that his fellow artists are solo players. If he is arbitrary, no matter how right he may be, he disturbs that fine feeling of artistic fellowship, that delicate balance of individual temperaments harmonized for and by a single purpose. In this connection I do not mind confessing that though I enjoy a good game of cards, I made it a rule never to play cards with my colleagues during the hours of railroad traveling involved in keeping our concert engagements. I played chess. In chess the element of luck does not enter. Each player is responsible for what he does or leaves undone. And defeat leaves no such sting as it does when all may be blamed on chance. In an *ensemble* that strives for perfection there must be no undercurrents of regret, of dissatisfaction—nothing that interferes with the sympathy and good will which makes each individual artist do his best. And so I have never regretted giving cards the go-by!"

HINTS TO THE SERIOUS VIOLIN STUDENT

Of late years Mr. Kneisel's activity as a teacher has added to his reputation. Few teachers can point to a galaxy of artist pupils which includes such names as Samuel Gardner, Sascha Jacobsen, Breskin, Helen Jeffry and Olive Meade (who perpetuates the ideals of his great string *ensemble* in her own quartet). "What is the secret of your method?" I asked him first of all. "Method is hardly the word," he told me. "It sounds too cut-and-dried. I teach according to principles, which must, of course, vary in individual cases; yet whose foundation is fixed. And like Joachim, or Leschetiszky, I have preparatory teachers.

THE GENERAL FAULT

"My experience has shown me that the fundamental fault of most pupils is that they do not know how to hold either the bow or the violin. Here in America the violin student as a rule begins serious technical study too late, contrary to the European practice. It is a great handicap to begin really serious work at seventeen or eighteen, when the flexible bones of childhood have hardened, and have not the pliability needed for violin gymnastics. It is a case of not bending the twig as you want the tree to grow in time. And those who study professionally are often more interested in making money as soon as possible than in bending all their energies on reaching the higher levels of their art. Many a promising talent never develops because its possessor at seventeen or eighteen is eager to earn money as an orchestra or 'job' player, instead of sacrificing a few years more and becoming a true artist. I've seen it happen time and again: a young fellow really endowed who thinks he can play for a living and find time to study and practice 'after hours.' And he never does!

"But to return to the general fault of the violin student. There is a certain angle at which the bow should cross the strings in order to produce those vibrations which give the roundest, fullest, most perfect tone [he took his own beautiful instrument out of its case to illustrate the point], and the violin must be so held that the bow moves straight across the strings in this manner. A deviation from the correct attack produces a scratchy

tone. And it is just in the one fundamental thing: the holding of
the violin in exactly the same position when it is taken up by the
player, never varying by so much as half-an-inch, and the correct
attack by the bow, in which the majority of pupils are deficient.
If the violin is not held at the proper angle, for instance, it is just
as though a piano were to stand on a sloping floor. Too many students play 'with the violin' on the bow, instead of holding the
violin steady, and letting the bow play.

"And in beginning to study, this apparently simple, yet funda-
mentally important, principle is often overlooked or neglected.
Joachim, when he studied as a ten-year-old boy under
Hellmesberger in Vienna, once played a part in a concerto by
Maurer, for four violins and piano. His teacher was displeased:
'You'll never be a fiddler!' he told him, 'you use your bow too
stiffly!' But the boy's father took him to Böhm, and he remained
with this teacher for three years, until his fundamental fault was
completely overcome. And if Joachim had not given his concentrated attention to his bowing while there was still time, he
would never have been the great artist he later became.

THE ART OF THE BOW

"You see," he continued, "the secret of really beautiful violin
playing lies in the bow. A Blondin crossing Niagara finds his wire
hard and firm where he first steps on it. But as he progresses it
vibrates with increasing intensity. And as the tight-rope walker
knows how to control the vibrations of his wire, so the violinist
must master the vibrations of his strings. Each section of the
string vibrates with a different quality of tone. Most pupils think
that a big tone is developed by pressure with the bow—yet
much depends on what part of the string this pressure is
applied. Fingering is an art, of course, but the great art is the art
of the bow, the 'art of bowing,' as Tartini calls it. When a pupil
understands it he has gone far.

"Every pupil may be developed to a certain degree without
ever suspecting how important a factor the manipulation of the
bow will be in his further progress. He thinks that if the fingers
of his left hand are agile he has gained the main end in view. But
then he comes to a stop—his left hand can no longer aid him,

and he finds that if he wants to play with real beauty of expression the bow supplies the only true key. Out of a hundred who reach this stage," Mr. Kneisel went on, rather sadly, "only some five or six, or even less, become great artists. They are those who are able to control the bow as well as the left hand. All real art begins with phrasing, and this, too, lies altogether in the mastery of bow—the very soul of the violin!"

I asked Mr. Kneisel how he came to write his own *Advanced Exercises* for the instrument. "I had an idea that a set of studies, in which each single study presented a variety of technical figures might be a relief from the exercises in so many excellent methods, where pages of scales are followed by pages of arpeggios, pages of double-notes and so forth. It is very monotonous to practice pages and pages of a single technical figure," he added. "Most pupils simply will not do it!" He brought out a copy of his "Exercises" and showed me their plan. "Here, for instance, I have scales, trills, arpeggios—all in the same study, and the study is conceived as a musical composition instead of a technical formula. This is a study in finger position, with all possible bowings. My aim has been to concentrate the technical material of a whole violin school in a set of *études* with musical interest."

And he showed me the second book of the studies, in ms., containing exercises in every variety of scale, and trill, bowing, *nuance,* etc., combined in a single musical movement. This volume also contains his own cadenza to the Beethoven violin concerto. In conclusion Mr. Kneisel laid stress on the importance of the student's hearing the best music at concert and recital as often as possible, and on the value and incentive supplied by a musical atmosphere in the home and, on leaving him, I could not help but feel that what he had said in our interview, his reflections and observations based on an artistry beyond cavil, and an authoritative experience, would be well worth pondering by every serious student of the instrument. For Franz Kneisel speaks of what he knows.

ADOLFO BETTI

THE TECHNIQUE OF THE MODERN QUARTET

What lover of chamber music in its more perfect dispensa-
tions is not familiar with the figure of Adolfo Betti, the
guiding brain and bow of the Flonzaley Quartet? Born in
Florence, he played his first public concert at the age of six, yet
as a youth found it hard to choose between literature, for which
he had decided aptitude,* and music. Fortunately for American
concert audiences of today, he finally inclined to the latter. An
exponent of what many consider the greatest of all violinistic
schools, the Belgian, he studied for four years with César
Thomson at Liège, spent four more concertizing in Vienna and
elsewhere, and returned to Thomson as the latter's assistant in
the Brussels Conservatory, three years before he joined the
Flonzaleys, in 1903. With pleasant recollections of earlier meet-
ings with this gifted artist, the writer sought him out, and found
him amiably willing to talk about the modern quartet and its
ideals, ideals which he personally has done so much to realize.

THE MODERN QUARTET

"You ask me how the modern quartet differs from its predecessors?" said Mr. Betti. "It differs in many ways. For one thing
the modern quartet has developed in a way that makes its inner
voices—second violin and viola—much more important than
they used to be. Originally, as in Haydn's early quartets, we

---

*M. Betti has published a number of critical articles in the *Guide Musical* of
Brussels, the *Rivista Musicale* of Turin, etc.

ADOLFO BETTI

à Monsieur Frederick H. Martens,
    souvenir d'estime et de sympathie.

New York. avril 1918.   Adolfo Betti

have a violin solo with three accompanying instruments. In Beethoven's last quartets the intermediate voices have already gained a freedom and individuality which before him had not even been suspected. In these last quartets Beethoven has already set forth the principle which was to become the basis of modern polyphony: '*first of all* to allow each voice to express itself freely and fully, and *afterward* to see what the relations were of one to the other.' In fact, no one has exercised a more revolutionary effect on the quartet than Beethoven—no one has made it attain so great a degree of progress. And surely the distance separating the quartet as Beethoven found it, from the quartet as he left it (*Grand Fugue,* Op. 131, Op. 132), is greater than that which lies between the *Fugue* Op. 132, and the most advanced modern quartet, let us say, for instance, Schoenberg's Op. 7. Schoenberg, by the way, has only applied and developed the principles established by Beethoven in the latter's last quartets. But in the modern quartet we have a new element, one which tends more and more to become preponderant, and which might be called *orchestral* rather than *da camera.* Smetana, Grieg, Tchaikovsky were the first to follow this path, in which the majority of the moderns, including Franck and Debussy, have followed them. And in addition, many among the most advanced modern composers *strive for orchestral effects that often lie outside the natural capabilities of the strings!*

"For instance Stravinsky, in the first of his three impressionistic sketches for quartet (which we have played), has the first violin play *ponticello* throughout, not the natural *ponticello,* but a quite special one, to produce an effect of a bag-pipe sounding at a distance. I had to try again and again till I found the right technical means to produce the effect desired. Then, the cello is used to imitate the drum; there are special technical problems for the second violin—a single sustained D, with an accompanying *pizzicato* on the open strings—while the viola is required to suggest the tramp of marching feet. And, again, in other modern quartets we find special technical devices undreamt of in earlier days. Borodin, for instance, is the first to systematically employ successions of harmonics. In the trio of his first quartet the melody is successively introduced by the cello and the first violin, altogether in harmonics.

THE MODERN QUARTET AND AMATEUR PLAYERS

"You ask me whether the average quartet of amateurs, of lovers of string music, can get much out of the more modern quartets. I would say yes, but with some serious reservations. There has been much beautiful music written, but most of it is complicated. In the case of the older quartets, Haydn, Mozart, etc., even if they are not played well, the performers can still obtain an idea of the music, of its thought content. But in the modern quartets, unless each individual player has mastered every technical difficulty, the musical idea does not pierce through, there is no effect.

"I remember when we rehearsed the first Schoenberg *Quartet*. It was in 1913, at a Chicago hotel, and we had no score, but only the separate parts. The results, at our first attempt, were so dreadful that we stopped after a few pages. It was not till I had secured a score, studied it and again tried it that we began to see a light. Finally there was not one measure which we did not understand. But Schoenberg, Reger, Ravel quartets make too great a demand on the technical ability of the average quartet amateur.

THE TECHNIQUE OF QUARTET PLAYING

"Naturally, the first violin is the leader, the Conductor of the quartet, as in its early days, although the 'star' system, with one virtuose player and three satellites, has disappeared. Now the quartet as a whole has established itself in the virtuoso field—using the word *virtuoso* in its best sense. The Müller quartet (Hanover), 1845–1850, was the first to travel as a chamber music organization, and the famous *Florentiner* Quartet the first to realize what could be done in the way of finish in playing. As *premier violiniste* of the Flonzaley I study and prepare the interpretation of the works we are to play before any rehearsing is done.

"While the first violin still holds first place in the modern quartet, the second violin has become much more important than formerly; it has gained in individuality. In many of the newer quartets it is quite as important as the first. In Hugo Wolf's quartet, for example, first and second violins are employed as though in a concerto for two violins.

"The viola, especially in modern French works—Ravel, Debussy, Samazeuil—has a prominent part. In the older quartets one reason the viola parts are simple is because the alto players as a rule were technically less skillful. As a general thing they were violinists who had failed—'the refugees of the G clef,' as Édouard Colonne, the eminent conductor, once wittily said. But the reason modern French composers give the viola special attention is because France now is ahead of the other nations in virtuose viola playing. It is practically the only country which may be said to have a 'school' of viola playing. In the Smetana *Quartet* the viola plays a most important part, and Dvořák, who himself played viola, emphasized the instrument in his quartets.

"Mozart showed what the cello was able to do in the quartets he dedicated to the 'cellist king,' Frederick William of Prussia. And then, the cello has always the musical importance which attaches to it as the lower of the two 'outer voices' of the quartet *ensemble*. Like the second violin and viola, it has experienced a technical and musical development beyond anything Haydn or Mozart would have dared to write.

REHEARSING

"Realization of the Art aims of the modern quartet calls for endless rehearsal. Few people realize the hard work and concentrated effort entailed. And there are always new problems to solve. After preparing a new score in advance, we meet and establish its general idea, its broad outlines in actual playing. And then, gradually, we fill in the details. Ordinarily we rehearse three hours a day, less during the concert season, of course; but always enough to keep absolutely in trim. And we vary our practice programs in order to keep mentally fresh as well as technically fit.

INTONATION

"Perfect intonation is a great problem—one practically

unknown to the average amateur quartet player. Four players
may each one of them be playing in tune, in pitch; yet their
chords may not be truly in tune, because of the individual bias—
a trifle sharp, a trifle flat—in interpreting pitch. This individual
bias may be caused by the attraction existing between certain
notes, by differences of register and *timbre,* or any number of
other reasons—too many to recount. The true beauty of the
quartet tone cannot be obtained unless there is an exact adjustment, a tempering of the individual pitch of each instrument, till
perfect accordance exists. This is far more difficult and complicated than one might at first believe. For example, let us take
one of the simplest violin chords," said Mr. Betti [and he rapidly set it down in pencil].

"Now let us begin by fixing the B so that it is perfectly in tune
with the E, then *without at all changing* the B, take the interval
D-B. You will see that the sixth will not be in tune. Repeat the
experiment, inverting the notes: the result will still be the same.
Try it yourself some time," added Mr. Betti with a smile, "and
you will see. What is the reason? It is because the middle B has
not been adjusted, tempered! Give the same notes to the first
and second violins and the viola and you will have the same
result. Then, when the cello is added, the problem is still more
complicated, owing to the difference in *timbre* and register. Yet
it is a problem which can be solved, and is solved in practically
everything we play.

"Another difficulty, especially in the case of some of the *very
daring* chords encountered in modern compositions, is the matter of balance between the individual notes. There are chords
which only *sound well* if certain notes are thrown into relief; and
others only if played very softly (almost as though they were
overtones). To overcome such difficulties means a great deal of
work, real musical instinct and, above all, great familiarity with
the composer's harmonic processes. Yet with time and patience
the true balance of tone can be obtained.

TEMPO

"All four individual players must be able to *feel* the tempo they are playing in the same way. I believe it was Mahler who once gave out a beat very distinctly—one, two, three—told his orchestra players to count the beat silently for twenty measures and then stop. As each *felt* the beat differently from the other, every one of them stopped at a different time. So *tempo,* just like intonation, must be 'tempered' by the four quartet players in order to secure perfect rhythmic inflection.

DYNAMICS

"Modern composers have wonderfully improved dynamic expression. Every little shade of meaning they make clear with great distinctness. The older composers, and occasionally a modern like Emanuel Moor, do not use expression marks. Moor says, 'If the performers really have something to put into my work the signs are not needed.' Yet this has its disadvantages. I once had an entirely unmarked sonata by Sammartini. As most first movements in the sonatas of that composer are *allegros* I tried the beginning several times as an *allegro,* but it sounded radically wrong. Then, at last, it occurred to me to try it as a *largo* and, behold, it was beautiful!

INTERPRETATION

"If the leader of the quartet has lived himself into and mastered a composition, together with his associates, the result is sure. I must live in the music I play just as an actor must live the character he represents. All higher interpretation depends on solving technical problems in a way which is not narrowly mechanical. And while the *ensemble* spirit must be preserved, the freedom of the individual should not be too much restrained. Once the style and manner of a modern composer are familiar, it is easier to present his works: when we first played the Reger quartet here some twenty years ago, we found pages which at first we could not at all understand. If one has fathomed Debussy, it is easier to play Milhaud, Roger-Ducasse, Samazeuil—for the music of the modern French school has much in common. One great cultural value the professional quartet has for the musical community is the fact that it gives a large circle a measure of acquaintance with the mode of thought and style of composers whose symphonic and larger works are often an unknown quantity. This applies to Debussy, Reger, the modern Russians, Bloch and others. When we played the Stravinsky pieces here, for instance, his *Petrushka* and *Firebird* had not yet been heard.

SOME IDEALS

"We try, as an organization, to be absolutely catholic in taste. Nor do we neglect the older music, because we play so much of the new. This year we are devoting special attention to the American composers. Formerly the Kneisels took care of them, and now we feel that we should assume this legacy. We have already played Daniel Gregory Mason's fine *Intermezzo,* and the other American numbers we have played include David Stanley Smith's *Second Quartet,* and movements from quartets by Victor Kolar and Samuel Gardner. We are also going to revive Charles Martin Loeffler's *Rhapsodies* for viola, oboe and piano.

"I have been for some time making a collection of sonatas *a tre,* two violins and cello—delightful old things by Sammartini, Leclair, the Englishman Boyce, Friedemann Bach and others. This is material from which the amateur could derive real enjoyment and profit. The Leclair sonata in D minor we have played some three hundred times; and its slow movement is one of the most beautiful *largos* I know of in all chamber music. The same thing could be done in the way of transcription for chamber music which Kreisler has already done so charmingly for the solo violin. And I would dearly love to do it! There are certain 'primitives' of the quartet—Johann Christian Bach, Gossec, Telemann, Michel Haydn—who have written music full of the rarest melodic charm and freshness. I have much excellent material laid by, but as you know," concluded Mr. Betti with a sigh, "one has so little time for anything in America."

HANS LETZ

THE TECHNIQUE OF BOWING

H ans Letz, the gifted Alsatian violinist, is well fitted to talk on any phase of his Art. A pupil of Joachim (he came to this country in 1908), he was for three years concertmaster of the Thomas orchestra, appearing as a solo artist in most of our large cities, and was not only one of the Kneisels (he joined that organization in 1912), but the leader of a quartet of his own. As a teacher, too, he is active in giving others an opportunity to apply the lessons of his own experience.

VIOLIN MASTERY

When asked for his definition of the term, Mr. Letz said: "There can be no such thing as an *absolute* mastery of the violin. Mastery is a relative term. The artist is first of all more or less dependent on circumstances which he cannot control—his mood, the weather, strings, a thousand and one incidentals. And then, the nearer he gets to his ideal, the more apt his ideal is to escape him. Yet, discounting all objections, I should say that a master should be able to express perfectly the composer's idea, reflected by his own sensitive soul.

THE KEY TO INTERPRETATION

"The bow is the key to this mastery in expression, in interpretation: in a lesser degree the left hand. The average pupil does not realize this but believes that mere finger facility is the whole gist of technique. Yet the richest color, the most delicate *nuance*, is mainly a matter of bowing. In the left hand, of course, the *vibrato* gives a certain amount of color effect, the intense, dramatic tone quality of the rapid *vibrato* is comparable on the violin to the *tremolando* of the singer. At the same time the *vibrato* used to excess is quite as bad as an excessive *tremolando* in the voice. But control of the bow is the key to the gates of the great field of declamation, it is the means of articulation and accent, it gives character, comprising the entire scale of the emotions. In fact, declamation with the violin bow is very much like declamation in dramatic art. And the attack of the bow on the string should be as incisive as the utterance of the first accented syllable of a spoken word. The bow is emphatically the means of expression, but only the advanced pupil can develop its finer, more delicate expressional possibilities.

THE TECHNIQUE OF BOWING

"Genius does many things by instinct. And it sometimes happens that very great performers, trying to explain some technical function, do not know how to make their meaning clear. With regard to bowing, I remember that Joachim (a master colorist with the bow) used to tell his students to play largely with the wrist. What he really meant was with an elbow-joint movement, that is, moving the bow, which should always be connected with a movement of the forearm by means of the elbow-joint. The ideal bow stroke results from keeping the joints of the right arm loose, and at the same time firm enough to control each motion made. A difficult thing for the student is to learn to draw the bow across the strings *at a right angle,* the only way to produce a good tone. I find it helps my pupils to tell them not to think of the position of the bow-arm while drawing the bow across the strings, but merely to follow with the tips of the fingers of the right hand an imaginary line running at a right angle across the strings. The whole bow then moves as it should, and the arm motions unconsciously adjust themselves.

RHYTHM AND COLOR

"Rhythm is the foundation of all music—not rhythm in its metronomic sense, but in the broader sense of proportion. I lay the greatest stress on the development of rhythmic sensibility in

the student. Rhythm gives life to every musical phrase." Mr.
Letz had a Brahms quartet open on his music stand. Playing the
following passage, he said:

"In order to give this phrase its proper rhythmic value, to
express it clearly, plastically, there must be a very slight separa-
tion between the sixteenths and the eighth-note following them.
This—the bow picked up a trifle from the strings—throws the
sixteenths into relief. As I have already said, tone color is for
the main part controlled by the bow. If I draw the bow above the
fingerboard instead of keeping it near the bridge, I have a decided contrast in color. This color contrast may always be established: playing near the bridge results in a clear and sharp tone,
playing near the fingerboard in a veiled and velvety one.

SUGGESTIONS IN TEACHING

"I find that, aside from the personal illustration absolutely
necessary when teaching, that an appeal to the pupil's imagination usually bears fruit. In developing tone-quality, let us say, I
tell the pupil his phrases should have a golden, mellow color, the
tonal equivalent of the hues of the sunrise. I vary my pictures
according to the circumstances and the pupil, in most cases,
reacts to them. In fast bowings, for instance, I make three color
distinctions or rather sound distinctions. There is the 'color of
rain,' when a fast bow is pushed gently over the strings, while
not allowed to jump; the 'color of snowflakes' produced when
the hairs of the bow always touch the strings, and the wood
dances; and 'the color of hail' (which seldom occurs in the classics), when in the real characteristic *spiccato* the whole bow
leaves the string."

THE ART AND THE SCHOOLS

In reply to another question, Mr. Letz added: "Great violin
playing is great violin playing, irrespective of school or nationality. Of course the Belgians and French have notable elegance,
polish, finish in detail. The French lay stress on sensuous beau-

ty of tone. The German temperament is perhaps broader, neglecting sensuous beauty for beauty of idea, developing the scholarly side. Sarasate, the Spaniard, is a unique national figure. The Slavs seem to have a natural gift for the violin—perhaps because of centuries of repression—and are passionately temperamental. In their playing we find that melancholy, combined with an intense craving for joy, which runs through all Slavonic music and literature. Yet, all said and done, Art is and remains first of all international, and the great violinist is a great artist, no matter what his native land."

DAVID MANNES

THE PHILOSOPHY OF VIOLIN TEACHING

That David Mannes, the well-known violinist and conductor, so long director of the New York Music School Settlement, would be able to speak in an interesting and authoritative manner on his art, was a foregone conclusion in the writer's mind. A visit to the educator's own beautiful "Music School" confirmed this conviction. In reply to some questions concerning his own study years Mr. Mannes spoke of his work with Heinrich de Ahna, Karl Halir and Eugène Ysaye. "When I came to de Ahna in Berlin, I was, unfortunately, not yet ready for him, and so did not get much benefit from his instruction. In the case of Halir, to whom I went later, I was in much better shape to take advantage of what he could give me, and profited accordingly. It is a point any student may well note—that when he thinks of studying with some famous teacher he be technically and musically equipped to take advantage of all that the latter may be able to give him. Otherwise it is a case of love's labor lost on the part of both. Karl Halir was a sincere and very thorough teacher. He was a Spohr player *par excellence*, and I have never found his equal in the playing of Spohr's *Gesangsscene*. With him I studied Kreutzer, Rode, Fiorillo; and to know Halir as a teacher was to know him at his best; since as a public performer—great violinist as he was—he did not do himself justice, because he was too nervous and high-strung.

STUDYING WITH YSAYE

"It was while sitting among the first violins in the New York

89

DAVID MANNES

Symphony Orchestra that I first heard Ysaye. And for the first time in my life I heard a man with whom I fervently *wanted* to study; an artist whose whole attitude with regard to tone and sound reproduction embodied my ideals.

"I worked with Ysaye in Brussels and in his cottage at Godinne. Here he taught much as Liszt did at Weimar, a group of from ten to twenty disciples. Early in the morning he went fishing in the Meuse, then back to breakfast and then came the lessons: not more than three or four a day. Those who studied drew inspiration from him as the pianists of the Weimar circle did from their Master. In fact, Ysaye's standpoint toward music had a good deal in common with Rubinstein's and he often said he wished he could play the violin as Rubinstein did the piano. Ysaye is an artist who has transcended his own medium—he has become a poet of sound. And unless the one studying with him could understand and appreciate this fact he made a poor teacher. But to me, in all humility, he was and will always remain a wonderful inspiration. As an influence in my career his marvelous genius is unique. In my own teaching I have only to recall his tone, his playing in his little cottage on the banks of the Meuse which the tide of war has swept away, to realize in a cumulative sense the things he tried to make plain to me then. Ysaye taught the technique of expression as against the expression of technique. He gave the lessons of a thousand teachers in place of the lessons of one. The greatest technical development was required by Ysaye of a pupil; and given this pre-requisite, he could open up to him ever enlarging horizons of musical beauty.

"Nor did he think that the true beauty of violin playing must depend upon six to eight hours of daily practice work. I absolutely believe with Ysaye that unless a student can make satisfactory progress with three hours of practice a day, he should not attempt to play the violin. Inability to do so is in itself a confession of failure at the outset. Nor do I think it possible to practice the violin intensively more than three-quarters of an hour at a time. In order to utilize his three hours of practice to the best advantage the student should divide them into four periods, with intervals of rest between each, and these rest periods might simply represent a transfer of energy—which is a rest in itself—to reading or some other occupation not necessarily germane to music, yet likely to stimulate interest in some other art.

SOME INITIAL PRINCIPLES OF VIOLIN STUDY

"The violin student first and foremost should accustom himself to practicing purely technical exercises without notes. The scales and arpeggios should never be played otherwise and books of scales should be used only as a reference. Quite as important as scale practice are broken chords. On the violin these cannot be played *solidly,* as on the piano; but must be studied as arpeggios, in the most exhaustive way, harmonically and technically. Their great value lies in developing an innate musical sense, in establishing an idea of tonality and harmony that becomes so deeply rooted that every other key is as natural to the player as is the key of C. Work of this kind can never be done ideally in class. But every individual student must himself come to realize the necessity of doing technical work without notes as a matter of daily exercise, even though his time be limited. Perhaps the most difficult of all lessons is learning to hold the violin. There are pupils to whom holding the instrument presents insurmountable obstacles. Such pupils, instead of struggling in vain with a physical difficulty, might rather take up the study of the cello, whose weight rests on the floor. That many a student was not intended to be a violin player by nature is proved by the various inventions, chin rests, braces, intended to supply what nature has not supplied. The study of the violin should never be allowed if it is going to result in actual physical deformity: raising of the left shoulder, malformation of the back, or eruptions resulting from chin rest pressure. These are all evidences of physical unfitness, or of incorrect teaching.

THE PHILOSOPHY OF VIOLIN TEACHING

"Class study is for the advanced student, not the beginner. In the beginning only the closest personal contact between the individual pupil and the teacher is desirable. To borrow an analogy from nature, the student may be compared to the young bird whose untrained wings will not allow him to take any trial flights unaided by his natural guardian. For the beginning violinist the principal thing to do is to learn the 'voice placing' of the violin. This goes hand in hand with the proper—which is the easy and natural—manner of holding the violin, bow study, and an appreciation of the acoustics of the instrument. The student's attention should at once be called to the marvelous and manifold qualities of the violin tone, and he should at once familiarize himself with the development of those contrasts of stress and pressure, ease and relaxation which are instrumental in its production. The analogies between the violin voice and the human voice should also be developed. The violin itself must to all intents become a part of the player himself, just as the vocal chords are part of the human body. It should not be considered a foreign tone-producing instrument adjusted to the body of the performer; but an extension, a projection of his physical self. In a way it is easier for the violinist to get at the chords of the violin and make them sound, since they are all exposed, which is not the case with the singer.

"There are two dangerous points in present-day standards of violin teaching. One is represented by the very efficient European professional standards of technique, which may result in an absolute failure of poetic musical comprehension. These should not be transplanted here from European soil. The other is the non-technical, sentimental, formless species of teaching which can only result in emotional enervation. Yet if forced to choose between the two the former would be preferable since without tools it is impossible to carve anything of beauty. The final beauty of the violin tone, the pure *legato,* remains in the beginning as in the end a matter of holding the violin and bow. Together they 'place' the tone just as the physical *media* in the throat 'place' the tone of the voice.

"Piano teachers have made greater advances in the tone developing technique of their instrument than the violin teachers. One reason is, that as a class they are more intellectual. And then, too, violin teaching is regarded too often as a mystic art, an occult science, and one into which only those specially gifted may hope to be initiated. This, it seems to me, is a fallacy. Just as a gift for mathematics is a special talent not given to all, so a *natural* technical talent exists in relatively few people. Yet this does not imply that the majority are shut off from playing the violin and playing it well. Any student who has music in his soul may be taught to play simple, and even relatively more difficult music with beauty, beauty of expression and interpretation. This he may be taught to do even though not endowed with a *natural* technical facility for the violin. A proof that natural technical facility is anything but a guarantee of higher musicianship is shown in that the musical weakness of many brilliant violinists, hidden by the technical elaboration of virtuoso pieces, is only apparent when they attempt to play a Beethoven *adagio* or a simple Mozart *rondo*.

"In a number of cases the unsuccessful solo player has a bad effect on violin teaching. Usually the soloist who has not made a success as a concert artist takes up teaching as a last resort, without enthusiasm or the true vocational instinct. The false standards he sets up for his pupils are a natural result of his own ineffectual worship of the fetish of virtuosity—those of the musical mountebank of a hundred years ago. Of course such false prophets of the virtuose have nothing in common with such high-priests of public utterance as Ysaye, Kreisler and others, whose virtuosity is a true means for the higher development of the musical. The encouragement of musicianship in general suffers for the stress laid on what is obviously technical *impedimenta*. But more and more, as time passes, the playing of such artists as those already mentioned, and others like them, shows that the real musician is the lover of beautiful sound, which technique merely develops in the highest degree.

"Today technique in a cumulative sense often is a confession of failure. For technique does not do what it so often claims to— produce the artist. Most professional teaching aims to prepare the student for professional life, the concert stage. Hence there is an intensive *technical* study of compositions that even if not wholly intended for display are primarily and principally projected for its sake. It is a well-known fact that few, even among gifted players, can sit down to play chamber music and do it justice. This is not because they cannot grasp or understand it; or because their technique is insufficient. It is because their whole violinistic education has been along the line of solo playing; they have literally been brought up, not to play *with* others, but to be accompanied *by* others.

"Yet despite all this there has been a notable development of violin study in the direction of *ensemble* work with, as a result, an attitude on the part of the violinists cultivating it, of greater humility as regards music in general, a greater appreciation of the charm of artistic collaboration: and—I insist—a technique both finer and more flexible. Chamber music—originally music written for the intimate surroundings of the home, for a small circle of listeners—carries out in its informal way many of the ideals of the larger orchestral *ensemble*. And, as regards the violinist, he is not dependent only on the literature of the string quartet; there are piano quintets and quartets, piano trios, and the duos for violin and piano. Some of the most beautiful instrumental thoughts of the classic and modern composers are to be found in the duo for violin and piano, mainly in the sonata form. Amateurs—violinists who love music for its own sake, and have sufficient facility to perform such works creditably—do not do nearly enough *ensemble* playing with a pianist. It is not always possible to get together the four players needed for the string quartet, but a pianist is apt to be more readily found.

"The combination of violin and piano is as a rule obtainable and the literature is particularly rich. Aside from sonatas by Corelli, Locatelli, Tartini, Bach, Mozart, Beethoven, Handel, Brahms and Schumann, nearly all the romantic and modern composers have contributed to it. And this music has all been written so as to show the character of each instrument at its best—the piano, harmonic in its nature; the violin, a natural melodic voice, capable of every shade of *nuance*." That Mr. Mannes, as an artist, has made a point of "practicing what he preaches" to the student as regards the *ensemble* of violin and piano will be recalled by all who have enjoyed the "Sonata Recitals" he has given together with Mrs. Mannes. And as an interpreting solo artist his views regarding the moot question of gut *versus* wire strings are of interest.

GUT VERSUS WIRE STRINGS

"My own violin, a Maggini of more than the usual size, dates from the year 1600. It formerly belonged to Dr. Leopold Damrosch. Which strings do I use on it? The whole question as to whether gut or wire strings are to be preferred may, in my opinion, be referred to the violin itself for decision. What I mean is that if Stradivarius, Guarnerius, Amati, Maggini and others of the old-master builders of violins had ever had wire strings in view, they would have built their fiddles in accordance, and they would not be the same we now possess. First of all there are scientific reasons against using the wire strings. They change the tone of the instrument. The rigidity of tension of the wire E string where it crosses the bridge tightens up the sound of the lower strings. Their advantages are: reliability under adverse climatic conditions and the incontestable fact that they make things easier technically. They facilitate purity of intonation. Yet I am willing to forgo these advantages when I consider the wonderful pliability of the gut strings for which Stradivarius built his violins. I can see the artistic retrogression of those who are using the wire E, for when materially things are made easier, spiritually there is a loss.

CHIN RESTS

"And while we are discussing the physical aspects of the instrument there is the 'chin rest.' None of the great violin makers ever made a 'chin rest.' Increasing technical demands, sudden pyrotechnical flights into the higher octaves brought the 'chin rest' into being. The 'chin rest' was meant to give the player a better grasp of his instrument. I absolutely disapprove, in theory, of chin rest, cushion or pad. Technical reasons may be adduced to justify their use, never artistic ones. I admit that progress in violin study is infinitely slower without the use of the pad; but the more close and direct a contact with his instrument the player can develop, the more intimately expressive his playing becomes. Students with long necks and thin bodies claim they have to use a 'chin rest,' but the study of physical adjustments could bring about a better coordination between them and the instrument. A thin pad may be used without much danger, yet I feel that the thicker and higher the 'chin rest' the greater the loss in expressive rendering. The more we accustom ourselves to mechanical aids, the more we will come to rely on them. . . . But the question you ask anent 'Violin Mastery' leads altogether away from the material!

VIOLIN MASTERY

"To me it signifies technical efficiency coupled with poetic insight, freedom from conventionally accepted standards, the attainment of a more varied personal expression along individual lines. It may be realized, of course, only to a degree, since the possessor of absolute 'Violin Mastery' would be forever glorified. As it is the violin master, as I conceive him, represents the embodier of the greatest intimacy between himself, the artist, and his medium of expression. Considered in this light Pablo Casals and his cello, perhaps, most closely comply with the requirements of the definition. And this is not as paradoxical as it may seem, since all string instruments are brethren, descended from the ancient viol, and the cello is, after all, a variant of the violin!"

TIVADAR NACHÉZ

JOACHIM AND LÉONARD AS TEACHERS

Tivadar Nachéz, the celebrated violin virtuoso, is better known as a concertizing artist in Europe, where he has played with all the leading symphonic orchestras, than in this country, to which he paid his first visit during these times of war, and which he was about to leave for his London home when the writer had the pleasure of meeting him. Yet, though he has not appeared in public in this country (if we except some Red Cross concerts in California, at which he gave his auditors of his best to further our noblest war charity), his name is familiar to every violinist. For is not Mr. Nachéz the composer of the *Gypsy Dances* for violin and piano, which have made him famous?

Genuinely musical, effective and largely successful as they have been, however, as any one who has played them can testify, the composer of the *Gypsy Dances* regards them with mixed feelings. "I have done other work that seems to me, relatively, much more important," said Mr. Nachéz, "but when my name happens to be mentioned, echo always answers '*Gypsy Dances*,' my little rubbishy '*Gypsy Dances*'! It is not quite fair. I have published thirty-five works, among them a *Requiem Mass*, an orchestral overture, two violin concertos, three rhapsodies for violin and orchestra, variations on a Swiss theme, Romances, a *Polonaise* (dedicated to Ysaye), and *Evening Song*, three *Poèmes hongrois*, twelve classical masterworks of the 17th century—to say nothing of songs, etc.—and the two concertos of Vivaldi and Nardini which I have edited, practically new creations, owing to the addition of the piano accompaniments and orchestral score.

TIVADAR NACHÉZ

I wrote the *Gypsy Dances* as a mere boy when I was studying with H. Léonard in Paris, and really at his suggestion. In one of my lessons I played Sarasate's *Spanish Dances,* which chanced to be published at the time, and at once made a great hit. So Léonard said to me: 'Why not write some *Hungarian* Gypsy dances—there must be wonderful material at hand in the music of the *Tziganes* of Hungary. You should do something with it!' I took him at his word, and he liked my 'Dances' so well that he made me play them at his musical evenings, which he gave often during the winter, and which were always attended by the musical *Tout Paris!* I may say that during these last thirty years there has been scarcely a violinist before the public who at one time or the other has *not* played these *Gypsy Dances.* Besides the *original* edition, there are two (pirated!) editions in America and six in Europe.

THE BEGINNING OF A VIOLINISTIC CAREER: PLAYING WITH LISZT

"No, Léonard was not my first teacher. I took up violin work when a boy of five years of age, and for seven years practiced from eight to ten hours a day, studying with Sabathiel, the leader of the Royal Orchestra in Budapest, where I was born, though England, the land of my adoption, in which I have lived these last twenty-six years, is the land where I have found all my happiness, and much gratifying honor, and of which I have been a devoted, ardent and loyal naturalized citizen for more than a quarter of a century. Sabathiel was an excellent routine teacher, and grounded me well in the fundamentals—good tone production and technical control. Later I had far greater teachers, and they taught me much, but—in the last analysis, most of the little I have achieved I owe to myself, to hard, untiring work: I had determined to be a violinist and I trust I became one. No serious student of the instrument should ever forget that, no matter who his teacher may be, he himself must supply the determination, the continued energy and devotion which will lead him to success.

"Playing with Liszt—he was an intimate friend of my father— is my most precious musical recollection of Budapest. I enjoyed it a great deal more than my regular lesson work. He would condescend to play with me some evenings and you can imagine what rare musical enjoyment, what happiness there was in playing with such a genius! I was still a boy when with him I played the Grieg *F major Sonata,* which had just come fresh from the press. He played with me the *D minor Sonata* of Schumann and introduced me to the mystic beauties of the Beethoven sonatas. I can still recall how in the Beethoven *C minor Sonata,* in the first movement, Liszt would bring out a certain broken chromatic passage in the left hand, with a mighty *crescendo,* an effect of melodious thunder, of enormous depth of tone, and yet with the most exquisite regard for the balance between the violin and his own instrument. And there was not a trace of condescension in his attitude toward me; but always encouragement, a tender affectionate and paternal interest in a young boy, who at *that moment* was a brother artist.

"Through Liszt I came to know the great men of Hungarian music of that time: Erkel, Hans Richter, Robert Volkmann, Count Geza Zichy, and eventually I secured a scholarship, which the king had founded for music, to study with Joachim in Berlin, where I remained nearly three years. Hubay was my companion there; but afterward we separated, he going to Vieuxtemps, while I went to Léonard.

JOACHIM AS A TEACHER AND INTERPRETER

"Joachim was, perhaps, the most celebrated teacher of his time. Yet it is one of the greatest ironies of fate that when he died there was not one of his pupils who was considered by the German authorities 'great' enough to take the place the Master had held. Henri Marteau, who was not his pupil, and did not even exemplify his style in playing, was chosen to succeed him! Henri Petri, a Vieuxtemps pupil who went to Joachim, played just as well when he came to him as when he left him. The same might be said of Willy Burmester, Hess, Kes and Halir, the latter one of those Bohemian artists who had a tremendous 'Kubelik-like' execution. Teaching is and always will be a special gift. There are many minor artists who are wonderful 'teachers,' and *vice versa!*

"Yet if Joachim may be criticized as regards the way of imparting the secrets of technical phases in his violin teaching, as a
teacher of interpretation he was incomparable! As an interpreter of Beethoven and of Bach in particular, there has never
been any one to equal Joachim. Yet he never played the same
Bach composition twice in the same way. We were four in our
class, and Hubay and I used to bring our copies of the sonatas
with us, to make marginal notes while Joachim played to us, and
these instantaneous musical 'snapshots' remain very interesting.
But no matter how Joachim played Bach, it was always with a
big tone, broad chords of an organ-like effect. There is no
greater discrepancy than the edition of the Bach sonatas published (since his death) by Moser, and which is supposed to
embody Joachim's interpretation. Sweeping chords, which
Joachim always played with the utmost breadth, are 'arpeggiat-
ed' in Moser's edition! Why, if any of his pupils had ever
attempted to play, for instance, the end of the *Bourée* in the
B minor Partita of Bach *à la Moser,* Joachim would have broken
his bow over their heads!

STUDYING WITH LÉONARD

"After three years' study I left Joachim and went to Paris.
Liszt had given me letters of introduction to various French
artists, among them Saint-Saëns. One evening I happened to
hear Léonard play Corelli's *La Folia* in the *Salle Pleyel,* and the
liquid clarity and beauty of his tone so impressed me that I
decided I must study with him. I played for him and he accepted me as a pupil. I am free to admit that my tone, which people
seem to be pleased to praise especially, I owe entirely to
Léonard, for when I came to him I had the so-called 'German
tone' *(son allemand),* of a harsh, rasping quality, which I tried to
abandon absolutely. Léonard often would point to his ears while
teaching and say: *'Ouvrez vos oreilles: écoutez la beauté du son!'*
('Open your ears: listen for beauty of sound!'). Most Joachim
pupils you hear (unless they have reformed) attack a chord with
the nut of the bow, the German method, which unduly stresses
the attack. Léonard, on the contrary, insisted with his pupils on
the attack being made with such smoothness as to be absolutely

unobtrusive. Being a nephew of Mme. Malibran, he attached special importance to the 'singing' tone, and advised his pupils to hear great singers, to *listen* to them, and to try and reproduce their *bel canto* on the violin.

"He was most particular in his observance of every *nuance* of shading and expression. He told me that when he played Mendelssohn's concerto (for the first time) at the Leipsic *Gewandhaus,* at a rehearsal, Mendelssohn himself conducting, he began the first phrase with a full *mezzo-forte* tone. Mendelssohn laid his hand on his arm and said: 'But it begins *piano!*' In reply Léonard merely pointed with his bow to the score—the *p* which is now indicated in all editions had been omitted by some printer's error, and he had been quite within his rights in playing *mezzo-forte*.

"Léonard paid a great deal of attention to scales and the right way to practice them. He would say, *'Il faut filer les sons: c'est l'art des maîtres.'* ('One must spin out the tone: that is the art of the masters.') He taught his pupils to play the scales with long, steady bowings, counting sixty to each bow. Himself a great classical violinist, he nevertheless paid a good deal of attention to virtuoso pieces; and always tried to prepare his pupils for *public life*. He had all sorts of wise hints for the budding concert artist, and was in the habit of saying: 'You must plan a program as you would the *ménu* of a dinner: there should be something for every one's taste. And, especially, if you are playing on a long program, together with other artists, offer nothing indigestible—let *your* number be a relief!'

SIVORI

"While studying with Léonard I met Sivori, Paganini's only pupil (if we except Catarina Caleagno), for whom Paganini wrote a concerto and six short sonatas. Léonard took me to see him late one evening at the *Hôtel de Havane* in Paris, where Sivori was staying. When we came to his room we heard the sound of slow scales, beautifully played, coming from behind the closed door. We peered through the keyhole, and there he sat on his bed stringing his scale tones like pearls. He was a little chap and had the tiniest hands I have ever seen. Was this a drawback? If so, no one could tell from his playing; he had a flawless technique, and a really pearly quality of tone. He was very jolly and amiable, and he and Léonard were great friends, each always going to hear the other whenever he played in concert. My four years in Paris were in the main years of storm and stress—plain living and hard, very hard, concentrated work. I gave some accompanying lessons to help keep things going. When I left Paris I went to London and then began my public life as a concert violinist.

GREAT MOMENTS IN AN ARTIST'S LIFE

"What is the happiest remembrance of my career as a virtuoso? Some of the great moments in my life as an artist? It is hard to say. Of course some of my court appearances before the crowned heads of Europe are dear to me, not so much because they were *court* appearances, but because of the graciousness and appreciation of the highly placed personages for whom I played.

"Then, what I count a signal honor, I have played no less than *three* times as a solo artist with the Royal Philharmonic Society of London, the oldest symphonic society in Europe, for whom Beethoven composed his immortal *9th Symphony* (once under Sir Arthur Sullivan's baton; once under that of Sir A. C. Mackenzie, and once with Sir Frederick Cowen as conductor— on this last occasion I was asked to introduce my new *Second Concerto in B minor,* Op. 36, at the time still in ms.). Then there is quite a number of great conductors with whom I have appeared, a few among them being Liszt, Rubinstein, Brahms, Pasdeloup, Sir August Manns, Sir Charles Hallé, L. Mancinelli, Weingartner and Hans Richter, etc. Perhaps, as a violinist, what I like best to recall is that as a boy I was invited by Richter to go with him to Bayreuth and play at the foundation of the Bayreuth festival theater, which however my parents would *not* permit owing to my tender age. I also remember with pleasure an episode at the famous Pasdeloup Concerts in the *Cirque d'hiver* in Paris, on an occasion when I performed the *F sharp minor Concerto* of Ernst. After I had finished, two ladies came to the green room: they were in deep mourning, and one of them

greatly moved, asked me to 'allow her to thank me' for the manner in which I had played this concerto—she said: *I am the
widow of Ernst!*' She also told me that since his death she had
never heard the concerto played as I had played it! In presenting to me her companion, the Marquise de Gallifet (wife of the
General de Gallifet who led the brigade of the *Chasseurs
d'Afrique* in the heroic charge of General Margueritte's cavalry
division at Sedan, which excited the admiration of the old king
of Prussia), I had the honor of meeting the once world famous
violinist Mlle. Millanollo, as she was before her marriage. Mme.
Ernst often came to hear me play her late husband's music, and
as a parting gift presented me with his beautiful 'Tourte' bow,
and an autographed copy of the first edition of Ernst's transcription for solo violin of Schubert's *Erlking*. It is so incredibly
difficult to play with proper balance of melody and accompaniment—I never heard any one but Kubelik play it—that it is
almost impossible. It is so difficult, in fact, that it should not be
played!

VIOLINS AND STRINGS: SARASATE

"My violin? I am a Stradivarius player, and possess two fine
Strads, though I also have a beautiful Joseph Guarnerius. Ysaye,
Thibaud and Caressa, when they lunched with me not long ago,
were enthusiastic about them. My favorite Strad is a 1716
instrument—I have used it for twenty-five years. But I cannot
use the wire strings that are now in such vogue here. I have to
have Italian gut strings. The wire E cuts my fingers, and besides
I notice a perceptible difference in sound quality. Of course,
wire strings are practical; they do not 'snap' on the concert
stage. Speaking of strings that 'snap,' reminds me that the first
time I heard Sarasate play the Saint-Saëns *Concerto*, at
Frankfort, he twice forgot his place and stopped. They brought
him the music, he began for the third time and then—the E
string snapped! I do not think *any* other than Sarasate could
have carried off these successive mishaps and brought his concert to a triumphant conclusion. He was a great friend of mine
and one of the most *perfect* players I have ever known, as well
as one of the greatest *grand seigneurs* among violinists. His ren-

dering of romantic works, Saint-Saëns, Lalo, Bruch, was exquisite—I have never, never heard them played as beautifully. On
the other hand, his Bach playing was excruciating—he played
Bach sonatas as though they were virtuoso pieces. It made one
think of Hans von Buelow's *mot* when, in speaking of a certain
famous pianist, he said: 'He plays Beethoven with velocity and
Czerny with expression.' But to hear Sarasate play romantic
music, his own *Spanish Dances* for instance, was all like glorious
birdsong and golden sunshine, a lark soaring heavenwards!

THE NARDINI CONCERTO IN A

"You ask about my compositions? Well, Eddy Brown is going
to play my *Second Violin Concerto,* Op. 36 in B flat, which I
wrote for the London Philharmonic Society, next season; Elman
the Nardini *Concerto in A,* which was published only shortly
before the outbreak of the war. Thirty years ago I found, by
chance, three old Nardini concertos for violin and bass in the
composer's *original* ms., in Bologna. The best was the one in
A—a beautiful work! But the bass was not even figured, and the
task of reconstructing the accompaniment for piano, as well as
for orchestra, and reverently doing justice to the composer's
original intent and idea; while at the same time making its beauties clearly and expressively available from the standpoint of the
violinist of today, was not easy. Still, I think I may say I succeeded." And Mr. Nachéz showed me some letters from famous
contemporaries who had made the acquaintance of this Nardini
concerto in A major. Auer, Thibaud, Sir Hubert Parry (who said
that he had "infused the work with new life"), Pollak,
Switzerland's ranking fiddler, Carl Flesch, author of the well-
known *Urstudien*—all expressed their admiration. One we cannot forbear quoting a letter in part. It was from Ottokar Sevčik.
The great Bohemian pedagogue is usually regarded as the
apostle of mechanism in violin playing: as the inventor of an
inexorably logical system of development, which stresses the
technical at the expense of the musical. The following lines
show him in quite a different light:

I would not be surprised if Nardini, Vivaldi and their companions were to appear to you at the midnight hour in order to thank the master for having given new life to their works, long buried beneath the mold of figured basses; works whose vital, pulsating possibilities these old gentlemen probably never suspected. Nardini emerges from your alchemistic musical laboratory with so fresh and lively a quality of charm that starving fiddlers will greet him with the same pleasure with which the bee greets the first honeyed blossom of spring.

VIOLIN MASTERY

"And now you want my definition of 'Violin Mastery'? To me the whole art of playing violin is contained in the reverent and respectful interpretation of the works of the great masters. I consider the artist only their messenger, singing the message they give us. And the more one realizes this, the greater becomes one's veneration especially for Bach's creative work. For twenty years I never failed to play the Bach solo sonatas for violin every day of my life—a violinist's 'daily prayer' in its truest sense! Students of Bach are apt, in the beginning, to play, say, the *finale* of the *G minor Sonata,* the final *Allegro* of the *A minor Sonata,* the *Gigue* of the *B minor,* or the *Preludio* of the *E major Sonata* like a mechanical exercise: it takes *constant* study to disclose their intimate harmonic melodious conception and poetry! One should always remember that technique is, after all, only a *means.* It must be acquired in order to be an unhampered master of the instrument, as a medium for presenting the thoughts of the great creators—but *these thoughts,* and not their medium of expression, are the chief objects of the true and great artist, whose aim in life is to serve his Art humbly, reverently and faithfully! You remember these words:

"'In the very torrent, tempest, and, as I may say, the whirlwind of passion, you must acquire and beget a temperance that may give it smoothness. Oh, it offends me to the soul to hear a robustious, periwig-pated fellow tear a passion to tatters, to very rags, to split the ears of the groundlings, who for the most part are capable of nothing but inexplicable dumbshows and noise! . . .'"

MAXIMILIAN PILZER

THE SINGING TONE AND THE VIBRATO

Maximilian Pilzer is deservedly prominent among younger American concert violinists. A pupil of Joachim, Shradieck, Gustav Hollander, he is, as it has already been picturesquely put, "a graduate of the rock and thorn university," an artist who owes his success mainly to his own natural gifts plus an infinite capacity for taking pains. Though primarily an interpreter his interlocutor yet had the good fortune to happen on Mr. Pilzer when he was giving a lesson. Essentially a solo violinist, Mr. Pilzer nevertheless has the born teacher's wish to impart, to share, where talent justifies it, his own knowledge. He himself did not have to tell the listener this—the lesson he was giving betrayed the fact.

It was Kreisler's *Tambourin Chinois* that the student played. And as Mr. Pilzer illustrated the delicate shades of *nuance,* of phrasing, of bowing, with instant rebuke for an occasional lack of "warmth" in tone, the improvement was instantaneous and unmistakable. The lesson over, he said:

THE SINGING TONE

"The singing tone is the ideal one, it is the natural violin tone. Too many violin students have the technical bee in their bonnet and neglect it. And too many believe that speed is brilliancy. When they see the black notes they take for granted that they must 'run to beat the band.' Yet often it is the teacher's fault if a good singing tone is not developed. Where the teacher's playing is cold, that of the pupil is apt to be the same. Warmth, round-ed fullness, the truly beautiful violin tone is more difficult to call forth than is generally supposed. And, in a manner of speaking, the soul of this tone quality is the *vibrato,* though the individual instrument also has much to do with the tone.

THE VIBRATO

"But not," Mr. Pilzer continued, "not as it is too often mistakenly employed. Of course, any trained player will draw his bow across the strings in a smooth, even way, but that is not enough. There must be an inner, emotional instinct, an electric spark within the player himself that sets the *vibrato* current in motion. It is an inner, psychic vibration which should be reflected by the intense, rapid vibration in the fingers of the left hand on the strings in order to give fluent expression to emotion. The *vibrato* can not be used, naturally, on the open strings, but otherwise it represents the true means for securing warmth of expression. Of course, some decry the *vibrato*—but the reason is often because the *vibrato* is too slow. One need only listen to Ysaye, Elman, Kreisler: artists such as these employ the quick, intense *vibrato* with ideal effect. An exaggerated *vibrato* is as bad as what I call 'the sentimental slide,' a common fault, which many violinists cultivate under the impression that they are playing expressively.

VIOLIN MASTERY AND ITS ATTAINMENT

"'Violin Mastery' expresses more or less the aspiration to realize an ideal. It is a hope, a prayer, rather than an actual fact, since nothing human is absolutely perfect. Ysaye, perhaps, with his golden tone, comes nearest to my idea of what 'Violin Mastery' should be, both as regards breadth and delicacy of interpretation. And guide-posts along the long road that leads to mastery of the instrument? Individuality in teaching, progress along natural lines, surety in bowing, a tone-production without forcing, cultivating a sense of rhythm and accent. I always remember what Moser once wrote in my autograph album: 'Rhythm and accent are the soul of music!'

THE SHINING GOAL

"And what a shining goal is waiting to be reached! The correct interpretation of Bach, Handel and the old Italian and French classics, and of the vast realm of *ensemble* music under which head come the Mozart and Beethoven violin sonatas, and those of their successors, Schumann, Brahms, etc. And aside from the classics, the moderns. And then there are the great violin concertos, in a class by themselves. They represent, in a degree, the utmost that the composer has done for the interpreting artist. Yet they differ absolutely in manner, style, thought, etc. Take Joachim's own Hungarian concerto, which I played for the composer, of which I still treasure the recollection of his patting me on the shoulder and saying: 'There is nothing for me to correct!' It is a work deliberately designed for technical display, and is tremendously difficult. But the wonderful Brahms concerto, those of Beethoven and Max Bruch; of Mozart and Mendelssohn—it is hard to express a preference for works so different in the quality of their beauty. The Russian Conus has a fine concerto in E, and Sinding a most effective one in A major. Edmund Severn, the American composer and violinist, has also written a notably fine violin concerto which I have played with the Philharmonic, one that ought to be heard oftener.

PLAYING BACH

"Bach is one of the most difficult of the great masters to interpret on the violin. His polyphonic style and interweaving themes demand close study in order to make the meaning clear. In the Bach *Chaconne,* for instance, some very great violinists do not pay enough attention to making a distinction between principal and secondary notes of a chord. Here [Mr. Pilzer took up a new Strad he has recently acquired and illustrated his meaning] in this four-note chord there is one important melody note which must stand out. And it can be done, though not without some study. Bach abounds in such pitfalls, and in studying him the closest attention is necessary. Once the problems involved overcome, his music gains its true clarity and beauty and the enjoyment of artist and listener is doubled.

MAUD POWELL

TECHNICAL DIFFICULTIES:
SOME HINTS FOR THE CONCERT PLAYER

Maud Powell is often alluded to as our representative "American *woman* violinist" which, while true in a narrower sense, is not altogether just in a broader way. It would be decidedly more fair to consider her a representative American violinist, without stressing the term "woman"; for as regards Art in its higher sense, the artist comes first, sex being incidental, and Maud Powell is first and foremost—an artist. And her infinite capacity for taking pains, her willingness to work hard have had no small part in the position she has made for herself, and the success she has achieved.

THE DEVELOPMENT OF A CONCERT VIOLINIST

"Too many Americans who take up the violin professionally," Maud Powell told the writer, "do not realize that the mastery of the instrument is a life study, that without hard, concentrated work they cannot reach the higher levels of their art. Then, too, they are too often inclined to think that if they have a good tone and technique that this is all they need. They forget that the musical instinct must be cultivated; they do not attach enough importance to musical surroundings: to hearing and understanding music of every kind, not only that written for the violin. They do not realize the value of *ensemble* work and its influence as an educational factor of the greatest artistic value. I remember when I was a girl of eight, my mother used to play the Mozart violin sonatas with me; I heard all the music I possi-

MAUD POWELL

bly could hear; I was taught harmony and musical form in direct connection with my practical work, so that theory was a living thing to me and no abstraction. In my home town I played in an orchestra of twenty pieces—Oh, no, not a 'ladies orchestra'— the other members were men grown! I played chamber music as well as solos whenever the opportunity offered, at home and in public. In fact music was part of my life.

"No student who looks on music primarily as a thing apart in his existence, as a bread-winning tool, as a craft rather than an art, can ever mount to the high places. So often girls (who some- times lack the practical vision of boys), although having studied but a few years, come to me and say: 'My one ambition is to become a great virtuoso on the violin! I want to begin to study the great concertos!' And I have to tell them that their first ambition should be to become musicians—to study, to know, to understand music before they venture on its interpretation. Virtuosity without musicianship will not carry one far these days. In many cases these students come from small inland towns, far from any music center, and have a wrong attitude of mind. They crave the glamor of footlights, flowers and applause, not realiz- ing that music is a speech, an idiom, which they must master in order to interpret the works of the great composers.

THE INFLUENCE OF THE TEACHER

"Of course, all artistic playing represents essentially the men- tal control of technical means. But to acquire the latter in the right way, while at the same time developing the former, calls for the best of teachers. The problem of the teacher is to prevent his pupils from being too imitative—all students are natural imita- tors—and furthering the quality of musical imagination in them. Pupils generally have something of the teacher's tone—Auer pupils have the Auer tone, Joachim pupils have a Joachim tone, an excellent thing. But as each pupil has an individuality of his own, he should never sink it altogether in that of his teacher. It is this imitative trend which often makes it hard to judge a young player's work. I was very fortunate in my teachers. William Lewis of Chicago gave me a splendid start. Then I studied in turn with Schradieck in Leipsic—Schradieck himself was a pupil of

Ferdinand David and of Léonard—Joachim in Berlin, and Charles Dancla in Paris. I might say that I owe most, in a way, to William Lewis, a born fiddler. Of my three European masters Dancla was unquestionably the greatest as a teacher—of course I am speaking for myself. It was no doubt an advantage, a decided advantage for me in my artistic development, which was slow—a family trait—to enjoy the broadening experience of three entirely different styles of teaching, and to be able to assimilate the best of each. Yet Joachim was a far greater violinist than teacher. His method was a cramping one, owing to his insistence on pouring all his pupils into the same mold, so to speak, of forming them all on the Joachim lathe. But Dancla was inspiring. He taught me De Bériot's wonderful method of attack; he showed me how to develop purity of style. Dancla's method of teaching gave his pupils a technical equipment which carried bowing right along, 'neck and neck' with the finger work of the left hand, while the Germans are apt to stress finger development at the expense of the bow. And without ever neglecting technical means, Dancla always put the purely musical before the purely virtuoso side of playing. And this is always a sign of a good teacher. He was unsparing in taking pains and very fair.

"I remember that I was passed first in a class of eighty-four at an examination, after only three private lessons in which to prepare the concerto movement to be played. I was surprised and asked him why Mlle. —— who, it seemed to me, had played better than I, had not passed. 'Ah,' he said, 'Mlle. —— studied that movement for six months; and in comparison, you, with only three lessons, play it better!' Dancla switched me right over in his teaching from German to French methods, and taught me how to become an artist, just as I had learned in Germany to become a musician. The French school has taste, elegance, imagination; the German is more conservative, serious, and has, perhaps, more depth.

TECHNICAL DIFFICULTIES

"Perhaps it is because I belong to an older school, or it may be because I laid stress on technique because of its necessity as a means of expression—at any rate I worked hard at it.

Naturally, one should never practice any technical difficulty too long at a stretch. Young players sometimes forget this. I know that *staccato* playing was not easy for me at one time. I believe a real *staccato* is inborn; a knack. I used to grumble about it to Joachim and he told me once that musically *staccato* did not have much value. His own, by the way, was very labored and heavy. He admitted that he had none. Wieniawski had such a wonderful *staccato* that one finds much of it in his music. When I first began to play his *D minor Concerto* I simply made up my mind to get a *staccato*. It came in time, by sheer force of will. After that I had no trouble. An artistic *staccato* should, like the trill, be plastic and under control; for different schools of composition demand different styles of treatment of such details.

"Octaves—the unison, not broken—I did not find difficult; but though they are supposed to add volume of tone they sound hideous to me. I have used them in certain passages of my arrangement of *Deep River*, but when I heard them played, promised myself I would never repeat the experiment. Wilhelmj has committed even a worse crime in taste by putting six long bars of Schubert's lovely *Ave Maria* in octaves. Of course they represent skill; but I think they are only justified in show pieces. Harmonics I always found easy; though whether they ring out as they should always depends more or less on atmospheric conditions, the strings and the amount of rosin on the bow. On the concert stage if the player stands in a draught the harmonics are sometimes husky.

THE AMERICAN WOMAN VIOLINIST
AND AMERICAN MUSIC

"The old days of virtuoso 'tricks' have passed—I should like to hope forever. Not that some of the old type virtuosos were not fine players. Remenyi played beautifully. So did Ole Bull. I remember one favorite trick of the latter's, for instance, which would hardly pass muster today. I have seen him draw out a long *pp*, the audience listening breathlessly, while he drew his bow way beyond the string, and then looked innocently at the point of the bow, as though wondering where the tone had vanished. It invariably brought down the house.

"Yet an artist must be a virtuoso in the modern sense to do his full duty. And here in America that duty is to help those who are groping for something higher and better musically; to help without rebuffing them. When I first began my career as a concert violinist I did pioneer work for the cause of the American woman violinist, going on with the work begun by Mme. Camilla Urso. A strong prejudice then existed against women fiddlers, which even yet has not altogether been overcome. The very fact that a Western manager recently told Mr. Turner with surprise that he 'had made a success of a woman artist' proves it. When I first began to play here in concert this prejudice was much stronger. Yet I kept on and secured engagements to play with orchestra at a time when they were difficult to obtain. Theodore Thomas liked my playing (he said I had brains), and it was with his orchestra that I introduced the concertos of Saint-Saëns (C min.), Lalo (F min.), and others, to American audiences.

"The fact that I realized that my sex was against me in a way led me to be startlingly authoritative and convincing in the masculine manner when I first played. This is a mistake no woman violinist should make. And from the moment that James Huneker wrote that I 'was not developing the feminine side of my work,' I determined to be just myself, and play as the spirit moved me, with no further thought of sex or sex distinctions which, in Art, after all, are secondary. I never realized this more forcibly than once, when, sitting as a judge, I listened to the competitive playing of a number of young professional violinists and pianists. The individual performers, unseen by the judges, played in turn behind a screen. And in three cases my fellow judges and myself guessed wrongly with regard to the sex of the players. When we thought we had heard a young man play it happened to be a young woman, and *vice versa*.

"To return to the question of concert-work. You must not think that I have played only foreign music in public. I have always believed in American composers and in American composition, and as an American have tried to do justice as an interpreting artist to the music of my native land. Aside from the violin concertos by Harry Rowe Shelly and Henry Holden Huss,

I have played any number of shorter original compositions by such representative American composers as Arthur Foote, Mrs. H. H. A. Beach, Victor Herbert, John Philip Sousa, Arthur Bird, Edwin Grasse, Marion Bauer, Cecil Burleigh, Harry Gilbert, A. Walter Kramer, Grace White, Charles Wakefield Cadman and others. Then, too, I have presented transcriptions by Arthur Hartmann, Francis Macmillan and Sol Marcosson, as well as some of my own. Transcriptions are wrong, theoretically; yet some songs, like Rimsky-Korsakov's *Song of India* and some piano pieces, like the Dvořák *Humoresque,* are so obviously effective on the violin that a transcription justifies itself. My latest temptative in that direction is my *Four American Folk Songs,* a simple setting of four well-known airs with connecting cadenzas—no variations, no special development! I used them first as *encores,* but my audiences seemed to like them so well that I have played them on all my recent programs.

SOME HINTS FOR THE CONCERT PLAYER

"The very first thing in playing in public is to free oneself of all distrust in one's own powers. To do this, nothing must be left to chance. One should not have to give a thought to strings, bow, etc. All should be in proper condition. Above all the violinist should play with an accompanist who is used to accompanying him. It seems superfluous to emphasize that one's program numbers must have been mastered in every detail. Only then can one defy nervousness, turning excess of emotion into inspiration.

"Acoustics play a greater part in the success of a public concert than most people realize. In some halls they are very good, as in the case of the Cleveland Hippodrome, an enormous place which holds forty-three hundred people. Here the acoustics are perfect, and the artist has those wonderful silences through which his slightest tones carry clearly and sweetly. I have played not only solos, but chamber music in this hall, and was always sorry to stop playing. In most halls the acoustic conditions are best in the evening.

"Then there is the matter of the violin. I first used a Joseph Guarnerius, a deeper toned instrument than the Jean Baptista

Guadagnini I have now played for a number of years. The Guarnerius has a tone that seems to come more from within the instrument; but all in all I have found my Guadagnini, with its glassy clearness, its brilliant and limpid tone-quality, better adapted to American concert halls. If I had a Strad in the same condition as my Guadagnini the instrument would be priceless. I regretted giving up my Guarnerius, but I could not play the two violins interchangeably; for they were absolutely different in size and tone-production, shape, etc. Then my hand is so small that I ought to use the instrument best adapted to it, and to use the same instrument always. Why do I use no chin rest? I use no chin rest on my Guadagnini simply because I cannot find one to fit my chin. One should use a chin rest to prevent perspiration from marring the varnish. My Rocca violin is an interesting instance of wood worn in ridges by the stubble on a man's chin.

"Strings? Well, I use a wire E string. I began to use it twelve years ago one humid, foggy summer in Connecticut. I had had such trouble with strings snapping that I cried: 'Give me anything but a gut string.' The climate practically makes metal strings a necessity, though some kind person once said that I bought wire strings because they were cheap! If wire strings had been thought of when Theodore Thomas began his career, he might never have been a conductor, for he told me he gave up the violin because of the E string. And most people will admit that hearing a wire E you cannot tell it from a gut E. Of course, it is unpleasant on the open strings, but then the open strings never do sound well. And in the highest registers the tone does not spin out long enough because of the tremendous tension: one has to use more bow. And it cuts the hairs: there is a little surface nap on the bow-hairs which a wire string wears right out. I had to have my four bows rehaired three times last season— an average of every three months. But all said and done it has been a God-send to the violinist who plays in public. On the wire A one cannot get the harmonics; and the aluminum D is objectionable in some violins, though in others not at all.

"The main thing—no matter what strings are used—is for the artist to get his audience into the concert hall, and give it a program which is properly balanced. Theodore Thomas first advised me to include in my programs short, simple things that my listeners could 'get hold of'—nothing inartistic, but something selected from their standpoint, not from mine, and played as artistically as possible. Yet there must also be something that is beyond them, collectively. Something that they may need to hear a number of times to appreciate. This enables the artist to maintain his dignity and has a certain psychological effect in that his audience holds him in greater respect. At big conservatories where music study is the most important thing, and in large cities, where the general level of music culture is high, a big solid program may be given, where it would be inappropriate in other places.

"Yet I remember having many recalls at El Paso, Texas, once, after playing the first movement of the Sibelius *Concerto*. It is one of those compositions which if played too literally leaves an audience quite cold; it must be rendered temperamentally, the big climaxing effects built up, its Northern spirit brought out, though I admit that even then it is not altogether easy to grasp.

VIOLIN MASTERY

"'Violin Mastery' or mastery of any instrument, for that matter, is the technical power to say exactly what you want to say in exactly the way you want to say it. It is technical equipment that stands at the service of your musical will—a faithful and competent servant that comes at your musical bidding. If your spirit soars 'to parts unknown,' your well trained servant 'technique' is ever at your elbow to prevent irksome details from hampering your progress. Mastery of your instrument makes mastery of your Art a joy instead of a burden. Technique should always be the hand-maid of the spirit.

"And I believe that one result of the war will be to bring us a greater self-knowledge, to the violinist as well as to every other artist, a broader appreciation of what he can do to increase and elevate appreciation for music in general and his Art in particular. And with these I am sure a new impetus will be given to the development of a musical culture truly American in thought and expression."

LEON SAMETINI

HARMONICS

L eon Sametini, at present director of the violin department of the Chicago Music College, where Sauret, Heermann and Sebald preceded him, is one of the most successful teachers of his instrument in this country. It is to be regretted that he has not played in public in the United States as often as in Europe, where his extensive *tournées* in Holland—Leon Sametini is a Hollander by birth—Belgium, England and Austria have established his reputation as a virtuoso, and the quality of his playing led Ysaye to include him in a quartet of artists "in order of lyric expression" with himself and Thibaud. Yet, the fact remains that this erstwhile *protégé* of Queen Wilhelmina—she gave him his beautiful Santo Serafin (1730) violin, whose golden varnish back "is a genuine picture,"—to quote its owner—is a distinguished interpreting artist besides having a real teaching gift, which lends additional weight to his educational views.

REMINISCENCES OF SEVČIK

"I began to study violin at the age of six, with my uncle. From him I went to Eldering in Amsterdam, now Willy Hess's successor at the head of the Cologne Conservatory, and then spent a year with Sevčik in Prague. Yet—without being his pupil—I have learned more from Ysaye than from any of my teachers. It is rather the custom to decry Sevčik as a teacher, to dwell on his absolutely mechanical character of instruction—and not without justice. First of all Sevčik laid all the stress on the left hand

and not on the bow—an absolute inversion of a fundamental principle. Eldering had taken great pains with my bow technique, for he himself was a pupil of Hubay, who had studied with Vieuxtemps and had his tradition. But Sevčik's teaching as regards the use of the bow was very poor; his pupils—take Kubelik with all his marvelous finger facility—could never develop a big bow technique. Their playing lacks strength, richness of sound. Sevčik soon noticed that my bowing did not conform to his theories; yet since he could not legitimately complain of the results I secured, he did not attempt to make me change it. Musical beauty, interpretation, in Sevčik's case were all subordinated to mechanical perfection. With him the study of some inspired masterpiece was purely a mathematical process, a problem in technique and mental arithmetic, without a bit of spontaneity. Ysaye used to roar with laughter when I would tell him how, when a boy of fifteen, I played the Beethoven *Concerto* for Sevčik—a work which I myself felt and knew it was then out of the question for me to play with artistic maturity—the latter's only criticisms on my performance were that one or two notes were a little too high, and a certain passage not quite clear.

"Sevčik did not like the Dvořák *Concerto* and never gave it to his pupils. But I lived next door to Dvořák at Prague, and meeting him in the street one day, asked him some questions anent its interpretation, with the result that I went to his home various times and he gave me his own ideas as to how it should be played. Sevčik never pointed his teachings by playing himself. I never saw him take up the fiddle while I studied with him. While I was his pupil he paid me the compliment of selecting me to play Sinigaglia's engaging *Violin Concerto,* at short notice, for the first time in Prague. Sinigaglia had asked Sevčik to play it, who said: 'I no longer play violin, but I have a pupil who can play it for you,' and introduced me to him. Sinigaglia became a good friend of mine, and I was the first to introduce his *Rapsodia Piedmontese* for violin and orchestra in London. To return to Sevčik—with all the deficiencies of his teaching methods, he had one great gift. He taught his pupils *how to practice!* And—aside from bowing—he made all mechanical problems, especially finger problems, absolutely clear and lucid.

A QUARTET OF GREAT TEACHERS
WITH WHOM ALL MAY STUDY

"Still, all said and done, it was after I had finished with all my teachers that I really began to learn to play violin: above all from Ysaye, whom I went to hear play wherever and whenever I could. I think that the most valuable lessons I have ever had are those unconsciously given me by four of the greatest violinists I know: Ysaye, Kreisler, Elman and Thibaud. Each of these artists is so different that no one seems altogether to replace the other. Ysaye with his unique personality, the immense breadth and sweep of his interpretation, his dramatic strength, stands alone. Kreisler has a certain sparkling scintillance in his playing that is his only. Elman might be called the Caruso among violinists, with the perfected sensuous beauty of his tone; while Thibaud stands for supreme elegance and distinction. I have learned much from each member of this great quartet. And if the artist can profit from hearing and seeing them play, why not the student? Every recital given by such masters offers the earnest violin student priceless opportunities for study and comparison. My special leaning toward Ysaye is due, aside from his wonderful personality, to the fact that I feel music in the same way that he does.

TEACHING PRINCIPLES

'My teaching principles are the results of my own training period, my own experience as a concert artist and teacher—before I came to America I taught in London, where Isolde Menges, among others, studied with me—and what either directly or indirectly I have learned from my great colleagues. In the Music College I give the advanced pupils their individual lessons; but once a week the whole class assembles—as in the European conservatories—and those whose turn it is to play do so while the others listen. This is of value to every student, since it gives him an opportunity of 'hearing himself as others hear him.' Then, to stimulate appreciation and musical development there are *ensemble* and string quartet classes. I believe that every violinist should be able to play viola, and in quartet work I make the players shift constantly from one to the other instrument in order to hear what they play from a different angle.

"For left hand work I stick to the excellent Sevčik exercises and for some pupils I use the Carl Flesch *Urstudien*. For studies of real *musical* value Rode, of course, is unexcelled. His studies are the masterpieces of their kind, and I turn them into concert pieces. Thibaud and Elman have supplied some of them with interesting piano accompaniments.

"For bowing, with the exception of a few purely mechanical exercises, I used Kreutzer and Rode, and Gavinies. Ninety-nine percent of pupils' faults are faults of bowing. It is an art in itself. Sevčik was able to develop Kubelik's left hand work to the last degree of perfection—but not his bowing. In the case of Kocian, another well-known Sevčik pupil whom I have heard play, his bowing was by no means an outstanding feature. I often have to start pupils on the open strings in order to correct fundamental bow faults.

"When watching a great artist play the student should not expect to secure similar results by slavish imitation—another pupil fault. The thing to do is to realize the principle behind the artist's playing, and apply it to one's own physical possibilities.

"Every one holds, draws and uses the bow in a different way. If no two thumb-prints are alike, neither are any two sets of fingers and wrists. This is why not slavish imitation, but intelligent adaptation should be applied to the playing of the teacher in the class-room or the artist on the concert-stage. For instance, the little finger of Ysaye's left hand bends inward somewhat—as a result it is perfectly natural for him to make less use of the little finger, while it might be very difficult or almost impossible for another to employ the same fingering. And certain compositions and styles of composition are more adapted to one violinist than to another. I remember when I was a student, that Wieniawski's music seemed to lie just right for my hand. I could read difficult things of his at sight.

DOUBLE HARMONICS

"Would I care to discuss any special feature of violin technique? I might say something anent double harmonics—a subject too often taught in a mechanical way, and one I have always taken special pains to make absolutely plain to my own pupils—for every violinist should be able to play double harmonics out of a clear understanding of how to form them.

"There are only two kinds of harmonics: natural and artificial. Natural harmonics may be formed on the major triad of each open string, using the open string as the tonic. As, for example, on the G string [and Mr. Sametini set down the following illustration]:

Then there are four kinds of artificial harmonics, only three of which are used: harmonics on the major third (1); harmonics on the perfect fourth (2); harmonics on the perfect fifth (3); and harmonics—never used—on the octave:

Where does the harmonic sound in each case? Two octaves and a third higher (1); two octaves higher (2); one octave and a fifth higher (3) respectively, than the pressed-down note. If the harmonic on the octave (4) were played, it would sound just an octave higher than the pressed-down note.

"Now say we wished to combine different double harmonics. The whole principle is made clear if we take, let us say, the first double-stop in the scale of C major in thirds as an example:

"Beginning with the lower of these two notes, the C, we find that it cannot not be taken as a natural harmonic because natural harmonics on the open strings run as follows: G, B, D on the G string; D, F sharp, A on the D string; A, C sharp, E on the A string; and E, G sharp, B on the E string. There are three ways of taking the C before mentioned as an artificial harmonic.

The E may be taken in the following manner:

     Nat. harmonic   Artificial harmonic

Now we have to combine the C and E as well as we are able. Rejecting the following combinations as *impossible*—any violinist will see why—

we have a choice of the two *possible* combinations remaining, with the fingering indicated:

"With regard to the *actual execution* of these harmonics, I advise all students to try and play them with every bit as much expressive feeling as ordinary notes. My experience has been that pupils do not pay nearly enough attention to the intonation of harmonics. In other words, they try to produce the harmonics *immediately*, instead of first making sure that both fingers are on the right spot before they loosen one finger on the string. For instance in the following: ▱ first play ▱ and then

▱ then loosen the fourth finger, and play ▱

"The same principle holds good when playing double harmonics. Nine tenths of the 'squeaking' heard when harmonics are played is due to the fact that the finger-placing is not properly prepared, and that the fingers are not on the right spot.

"Never, when playing a harmonic with an up-bow (∨), at the point, smash down the bow on the string; but have it already *on* the string *before* playing the harmonic. The process is reversed when playing a down-bow (⊓) harmonic. When beginning a harmonic at the frog, have the harmonic ready, then let the bow *drop* gently on the string.

"Triple and quadruple harmonics may be combined in exactly the same way. Students should never get the idea that you press down the string as you press a button and—presto—the magic harmonics appear! They are a simple and natural result of the proper application of scientific principles; and the sooner the student learns to form and combine harmonics himself instead of learning them by rote, the better will he play them. Too often a student can give the fingering of certain double harmonics and cannot use it. Of course, harmonics are only a detail of the complete mastery of the violin; but mastery of all details leads to mastery of the whole.

VIOLIN MASTERY

"And what is mastery of the whole? Mastery of the whole, real 'Violin Mastery,' I think, lies in the control of the interpretative problem, the power to awaken emotion by the use of the instrument. Many feel more than they can express, have more left hand than bow technique and, like Kubelik, have not the perfected technique for which perfected playing calls. The artist who feels beauty keenly and deeply and whose mechanical equipment allows him to make others feel and share the beauty he himself feels is in my opinion worthy of being called a master of the violin."

ALEXANDER SASLAVSKY

WHAT THE TEACHER CAN AND CANNOT DO

A lexander Saslavsky is probably best known as a solo artist, as the concertmaster of a great symphonic orchestra, as the leader of the admirable quartet which bears his name. Yet, at the same time, few violinists can speak with more authority anent the instructive phases of their Art. Not only has he been active for years in the teaching field; but as a pedagogue he rounds out the traditions of Ferdinand David, Massard, Auer, and Grün (Vienna *Hochschule*), acquired during his "study years," with the result of his own long and varied experience.

Beginning at the beginning, I asked Mr. Saslavsky to tell me something about methods, his own in particular. "Method is a flexible term," he answered. "What the word should mean is the cultivation of the pupil's individuality along the lines best suited to it. Not that a guide which may be employed to develop common-sense principles is not valuable. But even here, the same guide (violin-method) will not answer for every pupil. Personally I find De Bériot's *Violin School* the most generally useful, and for advanced students, Ferdinand David's second book. Then, for scales—I insist on my pupils being able to play a perfect scale through three octaves—the Hrimaly book of scales. Many advanced violinists cannot play a good scale simply because of a lack of fundamental work.

"As soon as the pupil is able, he should take up Kreutzer and stick to him as the devotee does to his Bible. Any one who can play the *42 Exercises* as they should be played may be called a well-balanced violinist. There are too many purely mechanical exercises—and the circumstance that we have Kreutzer, Rode, Fiorillo, Rovelli and Dont emphasizes the fact. And there are too many elaborate and complicated violin methods. Sevčik, for instance, has devised a purely mechanical system of this kind, perfect from a purely mechanical standpoint, but one whose consistent use, in my opinion, kills initiative and individuality. I have had experience with Sevčik pupils in quartet playing, and have found that they have no expression.

WHAT THE TEACHER CAN AND CANNOT DO

"After all, the teacher can only supply the pupil with the violinistic equipment. The pupil must use it. There is tone, for instance. The teacher cannot *make* tone for the pupil—he can only show him how tone can be made. Sometimes a purely physiological reason makes it almost impossible for the pupil to produce a good natural tone. If the finger-tips are not adequately equipped with 'cushions,' and a pupil wishes to use the *vibrato* there is nothing with which he can vibrate. There is real meaning, speaking of the violinist's tone, in the phrase 'he has it at his fingers' tips.' Then there is the matter of *slow* practice. It rests with the pupil to carry out the teacher's injunctions in this respect. The average pupil practices too fast, is too eager to develop his Art as a money maker. And too many really gifted students take up orchestra playing, which no one can do continuously and hope to be a solo player. Four hours of study work may be nullified by a single hour of orchestra playing. Musically it is broadening, of course, but I am speaking from the standpoint of the student who hopes to become a solo artist. An opera orchestra is especially bad in this way. In the symphonic *ensemble* more care is used; but in the opera orchestra they employ the *right* arm for tremolo! There is a good deal of *camouflage* as regards string playing in an opera orchestra, and much of the music—notably Wagner's—is quite impracticable.

"And lessons are often made all too short. A teacher in common honesty cannot really give a pupil much in half-an-hour—it is not a real lesson. There is a good deal to be said for class teaching as it is practiced at the European conservatories, especially as regards interpretation. In my student days I learned

much from listening to others play the concertos they had prepared, and from noting the teacher's corrections. And this even
in a purely technical way: I can recall Kubelik playing Paganini
as a wonderful display of the *technical* points of violin playing.

A GREAT DEFECT

"Most pupils seem to lack an absolute sense of rhythm—a
great defect. Yet where latent it may be developed. Here
Kreutzer is invaluable, since he presents every form of rhythmic
problem, scales in various rhythms and bowings. Kreutzer's
Exercise No. 2, for example, may be studied with any number of
bowings. To produce a broad tone the bow must move slowly,
and in rapid passages should never seem to introduce technical
exercises in a concert number. The student should memorize
Kreutzer and Fiorillo. Flesch's *Urstudien* offer the artist or professional musician who has time for little practice excellent
material; but are not meant for the pupil, unless he be so far
advanced that he may be trusted to use them alone.

TONE: PRACTICE TIME

"Broad playing gives the singing tone—the true violin tone—
a long bow drawn its full length. Like every general rule though,
this one must be modified by the judgment of the individual
player. Violin playing is an art of many mysteries. Some pupils
grasp a point at once; others have to have it explained seven or
eight different ways before grasping it. The serious student
should practice not less than four hours, preferably in twenty
minute intervals. After some twenty minutes the brain is apt to
tire. And since the fingers are controlled by the brain, it is best
to relax for a short time before going on. Mental and physical
control must always go hand in hand. Four hours of intelligent,
consistent practice work are far better than eight or ten of
fatigued effort.

A NATIONAL CONSERVATORY

"Some five years ago too many teachers gave their pupils the
Mendelssohn and Paganini concertos to play before they knew
their Kreutzer. But there has been a change for the better dur-

ing recent years. Kneisel was one of the first to produce pupils here who played legitimately, according to standard violinistic ideals. One reason why Auer has had such brilliant pupils is that poor students were received at the Petrograd Conservatory free of charge. All they had to supply was talent; and I look forward to the time when we will have a National conservatory in this country, supported by the Government. Then the poor, but musically gifted, pupil will have the same opportunities that his brother, who is well-to-do, now has.

SOME PERSONAL VIEWS AND REFLECTIONS

"You ask me to tell you something of my own musical preferences. Well, take the concertos. I have reached a point where the Mendelssohn, Mozart, Beethoven, Bach and Brahms concertos seen to sum up what is truly worth while. The others begin to bore me; even Bruch! Paganini, Wieniawski, etc., are mainly mediums of display. Most of the great violinists, Ysaye, Thibaud, etc., during recent years are reverting to the violin sonatas. Ysaye, for instance, has recently been playing the Lazzari sonata, a very powerful and beautiful work.

"My experiences as a 'concertmaster'? I have played with Weingartner; Saint-Saëns (whose amiability to me, when he first visited this country, I recall with pleasure); Gustav Mahler, Tchaikovsky, Safonoff, Seidel, Bauer, and Walter Damrosch, whose friend and associate I have been for the last twenty-two years. He is a wonderful man, many-sided and versatile; a notably fine pianist; and playing chamber music with him during successive summers is numbered among my pleasantest recollections.

"In speaking of concertos some time ago, I forgot to mention one work well worth studying. This is the Russian Mlynarski's *Concerto in D*, which I played with the Russian Symphony Orchestra some eight years ago for the first time in this country, as well as a fine *Romance and Caprice* by Rubinstein.

"Is the music a concertmaster is called upon to play always violinistic? Far from it. Symphonic music—in as much as the concertmaster is concerned, is usually not idiomatic violin music. Richard Strauss's *Violin Concerto* can really be played by the violinist. The *obbligatos* in his symphonies are a very different matter; they go beyond accepted technical boundaries. With Stravinsky it is the same. The violin *obbligato* in Rimsky-Korsakov's *Schéhérazade,* though, is real violin music. Debussy and Ravel are most subtle; they call for a particularly good ear, since the harmonic balance of their music is very delicate. The concertmaster has to develop his own interpretations, subject, of course, to the conductor's ideas.

VIOLIN MASTERY

"'Violin Mastery'? It means to me complete control of the fingerboard, a being at home in every position, absolute sureness of fingering, absolute equality of tone under all circumstances. I remember Ysaye playing Tchaikovsky's *Sérénade Mélancolique,* and using a fingering for certain passages which I liked very much. I asked him to give it to me in detail, but he merely laughed and said: 'I'd like to, but I cannot, because I really do not remember which fingers I used!' That is mastery—a control so complete that fingering was unconscious, and the interpretation of the thought was all that was in the artist's mind! Sevčik's 'complete technical mastery' is after all not perfect, since it represents mechanical and not mental control."

TOSCHA SEIDEL

HOW TO STUDY

Toscha Seidel, though one of the more recent of the young Russian violinists who represent the fruition of Professor Auer's formative gifts, has, to quote H. F. Peyser, "the transcendental technique observed in the greatest pupils of his master, a command of mechanism which makes the rough places so plain that the traces of their roughness are hidden to the unpracticed eye." He commenced to study the violin seriously at the age of seven in Odessa, his natal town, with Max Fiedemann, an Auer pupil. A year and a half later Alexander Fiedemann heard him play a De Bériot concerto in public, and induced him to study at the Stern Conservatory in Berlin, with Brodsky, a pupil of Joachim, with whom he remained for two years.

It was in Berlin that the young violinist reached the turning point of his career. "I was a boy of twelve," he said, "when I heard Jascha Heifetz play for the first time. He played the Tchaikovsky *Concerto,* and he played it wonderfully. His bowing, his fingering, his whole style and manner of playing so greatly impressed me that I felt I *must* have his teacher, that I would never be content unless I studied with Professor Auer! In 1912 I at length had an opportunity to play for the Professor in his home at Loschivitz, in Dresden, and to my great joy he at once accepted me as a pupil.

STUDYING WITH PROFESSOR AUER

"Studying with Professor Auer was a revelation. I had private lessons from him, and at the same time attended the classes at

132

Toscha Seidel

the Petrograd Conservatory. I should say that his great specialty, if one can use the word 'specialty' in the case of so universal a master of teaching as the Professor, was bowing. In all violin playing the left hand, the finger hand, might be compared to a perfectly adjusted technical machine, one that needs to be kept well oiled to function properly. The right hand, the bow hand, is the direct opposite—it is the painter hand, the artist hand, its phrasing outlines the pictures of music; its *nuances* fill them with beauty of color. And while the Professor insisted as a matter of course on the absolute development of finger mechanics, he was an inspiration as regards the right manipulation of the bow, and its use as a medium of interpretation. And he made his pupils think. Often, when I played a passage in a concerto or sonata and it lacked clearness, he would ask me: 'Why is this passage not clear?' Sometimes I knew and sometimes I did not. But not until he was satisfied that I could not myself answer the question, would he show me how to answer it. He could make every least detail clear, illustrating it on his own violin; but if the pupil could 'work out his own salvation' he always encouraged him to do so.

"Most teachers make bowing a very complicated affair, adding to its difficulties. But Professor Auer develops a *natural* bowing, with an absolutely free wrist, in all his pupils; for he teaches each student along the line of his individual aptitudes. Hence the length of the fingers and the size of the hand make no difference, because in the case of each pupil they are treated as separate problems, capable of an individual solution. I have known of pupils who came to him with an absolutely stiff wrist; and yet he taught them to overcome it.

ARTIST PUPILS AND AMATEUR STUDENTS

"As regards difficulties, technical and other, a distinction might be made between the artist and the average amateur. The latter does not make the violin his life work: it is an incidental. While he may reasonably content himself with playing well, the artist-pupil *must* achieve perfection. It is the difference between an accomplishment and an art. The amateur plays more or less for the sake of playing—the 'how' is secondary; but for the artist the 'how' comes first, and for him the shortest piece, a single scale, has difficulties of which the amateur is quite ignorant. And everything is difficult in its perfected sense. What I, as a student, found to be most difficult were double harmonics—I still consider them to be the most difficult thing in the whole range of violin technique. First of all, they call for a large hand, because of the wide stretches. But harmonics were one of the things I had to master before Professor Auer would allow me to appear in public. Some find tenths and octaves their stumbling block, but I cannot say that they ever gave me much trouble. After all, the main thing with any difficulty is to surmount it, and just *how* is really a secondary matter. I know Professor Auer used to say: 'Play with your feet if you must, but make the violin sound!' With tenths, octaves, sixths, with any technical frills, the main thing is to bring them out clearly and convincingly. And, rightly or wrongly, one must remember that when something does not sound out convincingly on the violin, it is not the fault of the weather, or the strings or rosin or anything else—it is always the artist's own fault!

HOW TO STUDY

"Scale study—all Auer pupils had to practice scales every day, scales in all the intervals—is a most important thing. And following his idea of stimulating the pupil's self-development, the Professor encouraged us to find what we needed ourselves. I remember that once—we were standing in a corridor of the Conservatory—when I asked him, 'What should I practice in the way of studies?' he answered: 'Take the difficult passages from the great concertos. You cannot improve on them, for they are as good, if not better, as any studies written.' As regards technical work we were also encouraged to think out our own exercises. And this I still do. When I feel that my thirds and sixths need attention I practice scales and original figurations in these intervals. But genuine, resultful practice is something that should never be counted by 'hours.' Sometimes I do not touch my violin all day long; and one hour with head work is worth any number of days without it. At the most I never practice more than three hours a day. And when my thoughts are fixed on other things it would be time lost to try to practice seriously. Without technical control a violinist could not be a great artist; for he could not express himself. Yet a great artist can give even a technical study, say a Rode *étude*, a quality all its own in playing it. That technique, however, is a means, not an end, Professor Auer never allowed his pupils to forget. He is a wonderful master of interpretation. I studied the great concertos with him—Beethoven, Bruch, Mendelssohn, Tchaikovsky, Dvořák, the Brahms *Concerto* (which I prefer to any other); the Vieuxtemps *Fifth* and Lalo (both of which I have heard Ysaye, that supreme artist who possesses all that an artist should have, play in Berlin); the Elgar *Concerto* (a fine work which I once heard Kreisler, an artist as great as he is modest, play wonderfully in Petrograd), as well as other concertos of the standard repertory. And Professor Auer always sought to have us play as individuals; and while he never allowed us to overstep the boundaries of the musically æsthetic, he gave our individuality free play within its limits. He never insisted on a pupil accepting his own *nuances* of interpretation because they were his. I know that when playing for him, if I came to a passage which demanded an especially beautiful *legato* rendering, he would say: 'Now show how you can sing!' The exquisite *legato* he taught was all a matter of perfect bowing, and as he often said: 'There must be no such thing as strings or hair in the pupil's consciousness. One must not play violin, one must sing violin!'

FIDDLE AND STRINGS

"I do not see how any artist can use an instrument which is quite new to him in concert. I never play any but my own Guadagnini, which is a fine fiddle, with a big, sonorous tone. As to wire strings, I hate them! In the first place, a wire E sounds distinctly different to the artist than does a gut E. And it is a difference which any violinist will notice. Then, too, the wire E is so thin that the fingers have nothing to take hold of, to touch firmly. And to me the metallic vibrations, especially on the open strings, are most disagreeable. Of course, from a purely practical standpoint there is much to be said for the wire E.

VIOLIN MASTERY

"What is 'Violin Mastery' as I understand it? First of all it means talent, secondly technique, and in the third place, tone. And then one must be musical in an all-embracing sense to attain it. One must have musical breadth and understanding in general, and not only in a narrowly violinistic sense. And, finally, the good God must give the artist who aspires to be a master good hands, and direct him to a good teacher!"

EDMUND SEVERN

THE JOACHIM BOWING AND OTHERS:
THE LEFT HAND

Edmund Severn's activity in the field of violin music is a three-fold one: he is a composer, an interpreting artist and a teacher, and his fortuitous control of the three vital phases of his Art make his views as regards its study of very real value. The lover of string music in general would naturally attach more importance to his *String Quartet in D major,* his *Trio* for violin, cello and piano, his *Violin Concerto in D minor,* the sonata, the *Oriental, Italian, New England* Suites for violin, and the fine *Suite in A major,* for two violins and piano, than to his symphonic poems for orchestra, his choral works and his songs. And those in search of hints to aid them to master the violin would be most interested in having the benefit of his opinions as a teacher, founded on long experience and keen observation. Since Mr. Severn is one of those teachers who are born, not made, and is interested heart and soul in this phase of his musical work, it was not difficult to draw him out.

THE JOACHIM BOWING

"My first instructor in the violin was my father, the pioneer violin teacher of Hartford, Conn., where my boyhood was passed, and then I studied with Franz Milcke and Bernard Listemann, concertmaster of the Boston Symphony Orchestra. But one day I happened to read a few lines reprinted in the *Metronome* from some European source, which quoted Wilhelmj as saying that Emanuel Wirth, Joachim's first assistant

at the Berlin *Hochschule,* 'was the best teacher of his genera-
tion.' This was enough for me: feeling that the best could be
none too good, I made up my mind to go to him. And I did.
Wirth was the viola of the Joachim Quartet, and probably a better teacher than was Joachim himself. Violin teaching was a cult
with him, a religion; and I think he believed God had sent him
to earth to teach fiddle. Like all the teachers at the *Hochschule*
he taught the regular 'Joachim' bowing—they were obliged to
teach it—as far as it could be taught, for it could not be taught
every one. And that is the real trouble with the 'Joachim' bowing. It is impossible to make a general application of it.

"Joachim had a very long arm and when he played at the point
of the bow his arm position was approximately the same as that
of the average player at the middle of the bow. Willy Hess was a
perfect exponent of the Joachim method of bowing. Why?
Because he had a very long arm. But at the *Hochschule* the
Joachim bowing was compulsory: they taught, or tried to teach,
all who came there to use it without exception; boys or girls
whose arms chanced to be long enough could acquire it, but big
men with short arms had no chance whatever. Having a medium long arm, by dint of hard work I managed to get my bowing
to suit Wirth; yet I always felt at a disadvantage at the point of
the bow, in spite of the fact that after my return to the United
States I taught the Joachim bowing for fully eight years.

"Then, when he first came here, I heard and saw Ysaye play,
and I noticed how greatly his bowing differed from that of
Joachim, the point being that his first finger was always in a position to press *naturally* without the least stiffness. This led me to
try to find a less constrained bowing for myself, working along
perfectly natural lines. The Joachim bowing demands a high
wrist; but in the case of the Belgian school an easy position at
the point is assumed naturally. And it is not hard to understand
that if the bow be drawn parallel with the bridge, allowing for
the least possible movement of hands and wrist, the greatest
economy of motion, there is no contravention of the laws of
nature and playing is natural and unconstrained.

"And this applies to every student of the instrument, whether
or not he has a long arm. While I was studying in Berlin,

Sarasate played there in public, with the most natural and unhampered grace and freedom in the use of his bow. Yet the entire *Hochschule* contingent unanimously condemned his bowing as being 'stiff'—merely because it did not conform to the Joachim tradition. Of course, there is no question but that Joachim was the greatest quartet player of his time; and with regard to the interpretation of the classics he was not to be excelled. His conception of Bach, Beethoven, Mozart, Brahms was wonderful. The insistence at the *Hochschule* on forcing the bowing which was natural to him on all others, irrespective of physical adaptability, is a matter of regret. Wirth was somewhat deficient in teaching left hand technique, as compared with, let us say, Schradieck. Wirth's real strength lay in his sincerity and his ability to make clear the musical contents of the works of the great masters. In a Beethoven or Spohr concerto he made a pupil give its due emphasis to every single note.

A PRE-TEACHING REQUISITE

"Before the violin student can even begin to study, there are certain pre-teaching requisites which are necessary if the teacher is to be of any service to him. The violin is a singing instrument, and therefore the first thing called for is a good singing tone. That brings up an important point—the proper adjustment of the instrument used by the student. If his lessons are to be of real benefit to him, the component parts of the instrument, post, bridge, bass-bar, strings, etc., must be accurately adjusted, in order that the sound values are what they should be.

"From the teaching standpoint it is far more important that whatever violin the student has is one properly built and adjusted, than that it be a fine instrument. And the bow must have the right amount of spring, of elasticity in its stick. A poor bow will work more harm than a poor fiddle, for if the bow is poor, if it lacks the right resilience, the student cannot acquire the correct bow pressure. He cannot play *spiccato* or any of the 'bouncing' bowings, including various forms of arpeggios, with a poor stick.

DRAWING A LONG BOW

"When I say that the student should 'draw a long bow,'" continued Mr. Severn with a smile, "I do not say so at a venture. If his instrument and bow are in proper shape, this is the next thing for the student to do. Ever since Tartini's time it has been acknowledged that nothing can take the place of the study of the long bow, playing in all shades of dynamics, from *pp* to *ff*, and with all the inflections of *crescendo* and *diminuendo*. Part of this study should consist of 'mute' exercises—not playing, but drawing the bow *above the strings,* to its full length, resting at either end. This ensures bow control. One great difficulty is that as a rule the teacher cannot induce pupils to practice these 'mute' exercises, in spite of their unquestionable value. All the great masters of the violin have used them. Viotti thought so highly of them that he taught them only to his favorite pupils. And even today some distinguished violinists play dumb exercises before stepping on the recital stage. They are one of the best means that we have for control of the violinistic nervous system.

WRIST-BOWING

"Wrist-bowing is one of the bowings in which the student should learn to feel absolutely and naturally at home. To my thinking the German way of teaching wrist-bowing is altogether wrong. Their idea is to keep the fingers neutral, and let the stick move the fingers! Yet this is wrong—for the player holds his bow at the finger-tips, that terminal point of the fingers where the tactile nerves are most highly developed, and where their direct contact with the bow makes possible the greatest variety of dynamic effect, and also allows the development of far greater speed in short bowings.

"Though the Germans say 'Think of the wrist!' I think with the Belgians: Put your mind where you touch and hold the bow, concentrate on your fingers. In other words, when you make your bow change, do not make it according to the Joachim method, with the wrist, but in the natural way, with the fingers always in command. In this manner only will you get the true wrist motion.

STACCATO AND OTHER BOWINGS

"After all, there are only two general principles in violin playing, the long and short bow, *legato* and *staccato*. Many a teacher finds it very difficult to teach *staccato* correctly, which may account for the fact that many pupils find it hard to learn. The main reason is that, in a sense, *staccato* is opposed to the nature of the violin as a singing instrument. To produce a true *staccato* and not a 'scratchato' it is absolutely necessary, while exerting the proper pressure and movement, to keep the muscles loose. I have evolved a simple method for quickly achieving the desired result in *staccato*. First I teach the attack in the middle of the bow, without drawing the bow and as though pressing a button: I have pupils press up with the thumb and down with the first finger, with all muscles relaxed. This, when done correctly, produces a sudden sharp attack.

"Then, I have the pupil place his bow in the middle, in position to draw a down-stroke from the wrist, the bow-hair being pressed and held against the string. A quick down-bow follows with an immediate release of the string. Repeating the process, use the up-stroke. The finished product is merely the combination of these two exercises—drawing and attacking simultaneously. I have never failed to give a pupil a good *staccato* by this exercise, which comprises the principle of all genuine *staccato* playing.

"One of the most difficult of all bowings is the simple up-and-down stroke used in the second Kreutzer *étude,* that is to say, the bowing between the middle and point of the bow, *tête d'archet,* as the French call it. This bowing is played badly on the violin more often than any other. It demands constant rapid changing and, as most pupils play it, the *legato* quality is noticeably absent. Too much emphasis cannot be laid on the truth that the 'singing stroke' should be employed for all bowings, long or short. Often pupils who play quite well show a want of true *legato* quality in their tone, because there is no connection between their bowing in rapid work.

"Individual bowings should always be practiced separately. I always oblige my pupils to practice all bowings on the open strings, and in all combinations of the open strings, because this allows them to concentrate on the bowing itself, to the exclusion of all else; and they advance far more quickly. Students should never be compelled to learn new bowings while they have to think of their fingers at the same time: we cannot serve two masters simultaneously! All in all, bowing is most important in violin technique, for control of the bow means much toward mastery of the violin.

THE LEFT HAND

"It is evident, however, that the correct use of the left hand is of equal importance. It seems not to be generally known that finger-pressure has much to do with tone-quality. The correct poise of the left hand, as conspicuously shown by Heifetz for instance, throws the extreme tips of the fingers hammerlike on the strings, and renders full-pressure of the string easy. Correctly done, a brilliance results, especially in scale and passage work, which can be acquired in no other manner, each note partaking somewhat of the quality of the open string. As for intonation—that is largely a question of listening. To really listen to oneself is as necessary as it is rare. It would take a volume to cover that subject alone. We hear much about the use of the *vibrato* these days. It was not so when I was a student. I can remember when it was laughed at by the purists as an Italian evidence of bad taste. My teachers decried it, yet if we could hear the great players of the past, we would be astonished at their frugal use of it.

"One should remember in this connection that there was a conflict among singers for many years as to whether the straight tone as cultivated by the English oratorio singers, or the vibrated tone of the Italians were correct. As usual, Nature won out. The correctly vibrated voice outlasted the other form of production, thus proving its lawful basis. But today the *vibrato* is frequently made to cover a multitude of violin sins.

"It is accepted by many as a substitute for genuine warmth and it is used as a *camouflage* to 'put over' some very bad art in the shape of poor tone-quality, intonation and general sloppiness of technique. Why, then, has it come into general use during the last twenty-five years? Simply because it is based on the correctly produced human voice. The old players, especially those of the German school, said, and some still say, the *vibrato* should only be used at the climax of a melody. If we listen to a Sembrich or a Bonci, however, we hear a vibration on every tone. Let us not forget that the violin is a singing instrument and that even Joachim said: 'We must imitate the human voice.' This, I think, disposes of the case finally and we must admit that every little boy or girl with a natural *vibrato* is more correct in that part of his tone-production than many of the great masters of the past. As the Negro pastor said: 'The world do move!'

VIOLIN MASTERY

"Are 'mastery of the violin' and 'Violin Mastery' synonymous in my mind? Yes and no: 'Violin Mastery' may be taken to mean that technical mastery wherewith one is enabled to perform any work in the entire literature of the instrument with precision, but not necessarily with feeling for its beauty or its emotional content. In this sense, in these days of improved violin pedagogy, such mastery is not uncommon. But 'Violin Mastery' may also be understood to mean, not merely a cold though flawless technique, but its living, glowing product when used to express the emotions suggested by the music of the masters. This latter kind of violin mastery is rare indeed.

"One who makes technique an end travels light, and should reach his destination more quickly. But he whose goal is music with its thousand-hued beauties, with its call for the exertion of human and spiritual emotion, sets forth on a journey without end. It is plain, however, that this is the only journey worth taking with the violin as a traveling companion. 'Violin Mastery,' then, means to me technical proficiency used to the highest extent possible, for artistic ends!"

ALBERT SPALDING

THE MOST IMPORTANT FACTOR
IN THE DEVELOPMENT OF AN ARTIST

For the duration of the war Albert Spalding the violinist became Albert Spalding the soldier. As First Lieutenant in the Aviation Service, U.S.A., he maintained the ideals of civilization on the Italian front with the same devotion he gave to those of Art in the piping times of peace. As he himself said not so very long ago: "You cannot do two things, and do them properly, at the same time. At the present moment there is more music for me in the factories gloriously grinding out planes and motors than in a symphony of Beethoven. And today I would rather run on an office-boy's errand for my country and do it as well as I can, if it's to serve my country, than to play successfully a Bach *Chaconne*; and I would rather hear a well directed battery of American guns blasting the Road of Peace and Victorious Liberty than the combined applause of ten thousand audiences. For it is my conviction that Art has as much at stake in this War as Democracy."

Yet Lieutenant Spalding, despite the arduous demands of his patriotic duties, found time to answer some questions of the writer in the interests of "Violin Mastery" which, representing the views and opinions of so eminent and distinctively American a violinist, cannot fail to interest every lover of the Art. Writing from Rome (Sept. 9, 1918), Lieutenant Spalding modestly said that his answers to the questions asked "will have to be simple and short, because my time is very limited, and then, too, having been out of music for more than a year, I feel it difficult to

145

ALBERT SPALDING

deal in more than a general way with some of the questions asked."

VIOLIN MASTERY

"As to 'Violin Mastery'? To me it means effortless mastery of details; the correlating of them into a perfect whole; the subjecting of them to the expression of an architecture which is music. 'Violin Mastery' means technical mastery in every sense of the word. It means a facility which will enable the interpreter to forget difficulties, and to express at once in a language that will seem clear, simple and eloquent, that which in the hands of others appears difficult, obtuse and dull.

THE MOST IMPORTANT FACTOR
IN THE DEVELOPMENT OF AN ARTIST

"As to the processes, mental and technical, which make an artist? These different processes, mental and technical, are too many, too varied and involved to invite an answer in a short space of time. Suffice it to say that the most *important* mental process, to my mind, is the development of a perception of beauty. All the perseverance in the study of music, all the application devoted to it, is not worth a tinker's dam, unless accompanied by this awakening to the perception of beauty. And with regard to the influence of teachers? Since all teachers vary greatly, the student should not limit himself to his own personal masters. The true student of Art should be able to derive benefit and instruction from every beautiful work of Art that he hears or sees; otherwise he will be limited by the technical and mental limitations of his own prejudices and jealousies. One's greatest difficulties may turn out to be one's greatest aids in striving toward artistic results. By this I mean that nothing is more fatally pernicious for the true artist than the precocious facility which invites cheap success. Therefore I make the statement that one's greatest difficulties are one's greatest facilities.

A LESS DEVELOPED PHASE OF VIOLIN TECHNIQUE

"In the technical field, the phase of violin technique which is less developed, it seems to me is, in most cases, bowing. One often notes a highly developed left hand technique coupled with a monotonous and oftentimes faulty bowing. The *color* and *variety* of a violinist's art must come largely from his intimate acquaintance with all that can be accomplished by the bow arm. The break or change from a down-bow to an up-bow, or *vice versa*, should be under such control as to make it perceptible only when it may be desirable to use it for color or accentuation.

GOOD AND BAD HANDS: MENTAL STUDY

"The influence of the physical conformation of bow hand and string hand on actual playing? There are no 'good' or 'bad' bow hands or string hands (unless they be deformed); there are only 'good' and 'bad' heads. By this I mean that the finest development of technique comes from the head, not from the hand. Quickness of thought and action is what distinguishes the easy player from the clumsy player. Students should develop mental study even of technical details—this, of course, in addition to the physical practice; for this mental study is of the highest importance in developing the student so that he can gain that effortless mastery of detail of which I have already spoken.

ADVANTAGE AND DISADVANTAGE
OF CONCERT ATTENDANCE FOR THE STUDENT

"Concerts undoubtedly have great value in developing the student technically and mentally; but too often they have a directly contrary effect. I think there is a very doubtful benefit to be derived from the present habit, as illustrated in New York, London, or other centers, of the student attending concerts, sometimes as many as two or three a day. This habit dwarfs the development of real appreciation, as the student, under these conditions, can little appreciate true works of art when he has crammed his head so full of truck, and worn out his faculties of concentration until listening to music becomes a mechanical mental process. The *indiscriminate* attending of concerts, to my mind, has an absolutely pernicious effect on the student.

NATIONALITY AS A FORMATIVE INFLUENCE

"Nationality and national feeling have a very real influence in the development of an artist; but this influence is felt subconsciously more than consciously, and it reacts more on the creative than on the interpretative artist. By this I mean that the interpretative artist, while reserving the right to his individual expression, should subject himself to what he considers to have been the artistic impulse, the artistic intentions of the composer. As to the type of music to whose appeal I as an American am susceptible, I confess to a very sympathetic reaction to the syncopated rhythms known as 'rag-time,' and which appear to be especially American in character." For the benefit of those readers who may not chance to know it, Lieutenant Spalding's *Alabama,* a Southern melody and dance in plantation style, for violin and piano, represents a very delightful creative exploitation of these rhythms. The writer makes mention of the fact since with regard to this and other of his own compositions Lieutenant Spalding would only state: "I felt that I had something to say and, therefore, tried to say it. Whether what I have to say is of any interest to others is not for me to judge.

PLAYING WHILE IN SERVICE

"Do I play at all while in Service? I gave up all playing in public when entering the Army a year ago, and to a great extent all private playing as well. I have on one or two occasions played at charity concerts during the past year, once in Rome, and once in the little town in Italy near the aviation camp at which I was stationed at the time. I have purposely refused all other requests to play because one cannot do two things at once, and do them properly. My time now belongs to my country: When we have peace again I shall hope once more to devote it to Art."

THEODORE SPIERING

THE APPLICATION OF BOW EXERCISES
TO THE STUDY OF KREUTZER

A. Walter Kramer has said: "Mr. Spiering knows how serious a study can be made of the violin, because he has made it. He has investigated the 'how' and 'why' of every detail, and what he has to say about the violin is the utterance of a big musician, one who has mastered the instrument." And Theodore Spiering, solo artist and conductor, as a teacher has that wider horizon which has justified the statement made that "he is animated by the thoughts and ideals which stimulate a Godowsky or Busoni." Such being the case, it was with unmixed satisfaction that the writer found Mr. Spiering willing to give him the benefit of some of those constructive ideas of his as regards violin study which have established his reputation so prominently in that field.

TWO TYPES OF STUDENTS

"There are certain underlying principles which govern every detail of the violinist's Art," said Mr. Spiering, "and unless the violinist fully appreciates their significance, and has the intelligence and patience to apply them in everything he does, he will never achieve that absolute command over his instrument which mastery implies.

"It is a peculiar fact that a large percentage of students—probably believing that they can reach their goal by a short cut—resent the mental effort required to master these principles, the passive resistance, evident in their work, preventing

150

THEODORE SPIERING

them from deriving true benefit from their studies. They form that large class which learns merely by imitation, and invariably retrograde the moment they are no longer under the teacher's supervision.

"The smaller group, with an analytical bent of mind, largely subject themselves to the needed mental drill and thus provide for themselves that inestimable basic quality that makes them independent and capable of developing their talent to its full fruition.

MENTAL AND PHYSICAL PROCESSES COORDINATED

"The conventional manner of teaching provided an inordinate number of mechanical exercises in order to overcome so called 'technical difficulties.' Only the *prima facie* disturbance, however, was thus taken into consideration—not its actual cause. The result was, that notwithstanding the great amount of labor thus expended, the effort had to be repeated each time the problem was confronted. Aside from the obviously uncertain results secured in this manner, it meant deadening of the imagination and cramping of interpretative possibilities. It is only possible to reduce to a minimum the element of chance by scrupulously carrying out the dictates of the laws governing vital principles. Analysis and the severest self-criticism are the means of determination as to whether theory and practice conform with one another.

"*Mental preparedness* (Marcus Aurelius calls it 'the good ordering of the mind') is the keynote of technical control. Together with the principle of *relaxation* it provides the player with the most effective means of establishing precise and sensitive cooperation between mental and physical processes. Muscular relaxation at will is one of the results of this cooperation. It makes sustained effort possible (counteracting the contraction ordinarily resulting therefrom), and it is freedom of movement more than anything else that tends to establish confidence.

THE TWO-FOLD VALUE
OF CELEBRATED STUDY WORKS

"The study period of the average American is limited. It has been growing less year by year. Hence the teacher has had to redouble his efforts. The desire to give my pupils the essentials of technical control in their most concentrated and immediately applicable form, have led me to evolve a series of 'bow exercises,' which, however, do not merely pursue a mechanical purpose. Primarily enforcing the carrying out of basic principles as pertaining to the bow—and establishing or correcting (as the case may be) arm and hand (right arm) positions, they supply the means of creating a larger interpretative style.

"I use the Kreutzer studies as the medium of these bow exercises, since the application of new technical ideas is easier when the music itself is familiar to the student. I have a two-fold object in mind when I review these studies in my particular manner, technique and appreciation. I might add that not only Kreutzer, but Fiorillo and Rode—in fact all the celebrated *Caprices*, with the possible exception of those of Paganini—are viewed almost entirely from the purely technical side, as belonging to the classroom, because their musical qualities have not been sufficiently pointed out. Rode, in particular, is a veritable musical treasure trove.

THE APPLICATION OF BOW EXERCISES
TO THE STUDY OF KREUTZER

"How do I use the Kreutzer studies to develop style and technique? By making the student study them in such wise that the following principles are emphasized in his work: *control before action* (mental direction at all times); *relaxation*; and *observance of string levels*; for unimpeded movement is more important than pressure as regards the carrying tone. These principles are among the most important pertaining to right arm technique.

"In *Study No. 2* (version 1, up-strokes only, version 2, down-strokes only), I have my pupils use the full arm stroke (*grand detaché*). In version 1, the bow is taken from the string after completion of stroke—but in such a way that the vibrations of the string are not interfered with. Complete relaxation is insured by release of the thumb—the bow being caught in a casual manner, third and fourth fingers slipping from their normal position on stick—and holding, but not tightly clasping, the bow.

"Version 2 calls for a *return down-stroke*, the return part of the stroke being accomplished over the string, but making no division in stroke, no hesitating before the return. Relaxation is secured as before. Rapidity of stroke, elimination of impediment (faulty hand or arm position and unnecessary upper arm action), is the aim of this exercise. The pause between each stroke—caused by relinquishing the hold on the bow—reminds the student that mental control should at all times be paramount: that analysis of technical detail is of vital importance.

"In *Study No. 7* I employ the same vigorous full arm strokes as in *No. 2*: the up and down bows as indicated in the original version. The bow is raised from the strings after each note, by means of hand (little finger, first and thumb) not by arm action. Normal hand position is retained: thumb not released.

"The *observance of string levels* is very essential. While the stroke is in progress the arm must not leave its level in an anticipatory movement to reach the next level. Especially after the down-stroke is it advisable to verify the arm position with regard to this feature.

"*No. 8* affords opportunity for a *résumé* of the work done in *Nos. 2* and *7*:

"It is evident that the tempo of this study must be very much reduced in speed. The *return* down-stroke as in *No. 2*: the *second* down-stroke as in *No. 7*: the up-strokes as in *No. 2*.

"In *Study No. 5* I use the hand-stroke only—at the frog—arm absolutely immobile, with no attempt at tone. This exercise represents the first attempt at dissecting the *martelé* idea: precise timing of pressure, movement (stroke), and relaxation. The pause between the strokes is utilized to learn the value of left hand preparedness, with the fingers in place before bow action.

"In *Study No. 13* I develop the principles of string crossing, of the extension stroke, and articulation. String crossing is the main feature of the exercise. I employ three versions, in order to accomplish my aim. In version 1 I consider only the crossing from a higher to a lower level:

version 2:

version 3 is the original version. In versions 1 and 2 I omit all repetitions:

Articulation is one of the main points at issue—the middle note is generally inarticulate. For further string crossing analysis I use Kreutzer's *No. 25. Study No. 10* I carry out as a *martelé* study, with the string crossing very much in evidence; establishing observance of the notes occurring on the same string level, consequently compelling a more judicious use of the so-called wrist movement (not merely developing a supple wrist, with indefinite crossing movements, which in many cases are applied by the player without regard to actual string crossing) and in consequence securing stability of bow on string when string level is not changed, this result being secured even in rapid passage work.

"In *Studies 11, 19* and *21* I cover shifting and left thumb action: in *No. 9*, finger action—flexibility and evenness, the left thumb relaxed—the fundamental idea of the trill. After the *interrupted* types of bowing (grand *detaché, martelé, staccato*) have been carefully studied, the *continuous* types (*detaché, legato* and *spiccato*) are then taken up, and in part the same studies again used: *2, 7, 8*. Lastly the slurred *legato* comes under consideration (*Studies 9, 11, 14, 22, 27, 29*). Shifting, extension and string crossing have all been previously considered, and hence the *legato* should be allowed to take its even course.

"Although I do, temporarily, place these studies on a purely mechanical level, I am convinced that they thus serve to call into being a broader *musical* appreciation for the whole set. For I have found that in spite of the fact that pupils who come to me have all played their Kreutzer, with very few exceptions have they realized the musical message which it contains. The time when the student body will have learned to depict successfully musical character—even in studies and caprices—will mark the fulfillment of the teacher's task with regard to the cultivation of the right arm—which is essentially the teacher's domain.

SOME OF MR. SPIERING'S OWN STUDY SOUVENIRS

"It may interest you to know," Mr. Spiering said in reply to a question, "that I began my teaching career in Chicago immediately following my four years with Joachim in Berlin. It was natural that I should first commit myself to the pedagogic methods of the *Hochschule*, which to a great extent, however, I discarded as my own views crystallized. I found that too much emphasis allotted the wrist-stroke (a misnomer, by the way), was bound to result in too academic a style. By transferring primary importance to the control of the full arm-stroke—with the hand-stroke incidentally completing the control—I felt that I was better able to reflect the larger interpretative ideals which my years of musical development were creating for me. Chamber music—a youthful passion—led me to interest myself in symphonic work and conducting. These activities not only reacted favorably on my solo playing, but influenced my development as regards the broader, more dramatic style, the grand manner in interpretation. It is this realization that places me in a position to earnestly advise the ambitious student not to disregard the great artistic benefits to be derived from the cultivation of chamber music and symphonic playing.

"I might call my teaching ideals a combination of those of the Franco-Belgian and German schools. To the former I attribute my preference for the large sweep of the bow-arm, its style and tonal superiority; to the latter, vigor of interpretation and attention to musical detail.

VIOLIN MASTERY

"How do I define 'Violin Mastery'? The violinist who has succeeded in eliminating all superfluous tension or physical resistance, whose mental control is such that the technique of the left hand and right arm has become coordinate, thus forming a perfect mechanism not working at cross-purposes; who, furthermore, is so well poised that he never oversteps the boundaries of good taste in his interpretations, though vitally alive to the human element; who, finally, has so broad an outlook on life and Art that he is able to reveal the transcendent spirit characterizing the works of the great masters—such a violinist has truly attained mastery!"

JACQUES THIBAUD

THE IDEAL PROGRAM

Jacques Thibaud, whose gifts as an interpreting artist have brought him so many friends and admirers in the United States, is the foremost representative of the modern French school of violin-playing. And as such he has held his own ever since, at the age of twenty, he resigned his rank as concertmaster of the Colonne orchestra, to dedicate his talents exclusively to the concert stage. So great an authority as the last edition of the Riemann *Musik-Lexicon* cannot forbear, even in 1915, to emphasize his "technique, absolutely developed in its every detail, and his fiery and poetic manner of interpretation."

But Mr. Thibaud does not see any great difference between the ideals of *la grande école belge,* that of Vieuxtemps, De Bériot, Léonard, Massart and Marsick, whose greatest present-day exponent is Eugène Ysaye, and the French. Himself a pupil of Marsick, he inherited the French traditions of Alard through his father, who was Alard's pupil and handed them on to his son. "The two schools have married and are as one," declared Mr. Thibaud. "They may differ in the interpretation of music, but to me they seem to have merged so far as their systems of finger technique, bowing and tone production goes.

THE GREATEST DIFFICULTY TO OVERCOME

"You ask me what is most difficult in playing the violin? It is bowing. Bowing makes up approximately eighty percent of the sum total of violinistic difficulties. One reason for it is that many teachers with excellent ideas on the subject present it to their

JACQUES THIBAUD

pupils in too complicated a manner. The bow must be used in an absolutely natural way, and over elaboration in explaining what should be a simple and natural development often prevents the student from securing a good bowing, the end in view. Sarasate (he was an intimate friend of mine) always used his bow in the most natural way, his control of it was unsought and unconscious. Were I a teacher I should not say: 'You must bow as I do'; but rather: 'Find the way of bowing most convenient and natural to you and use it!' Bowing is largely a physical and individual matter. I am slender but have long, large fingers; Kreisler is a larger man than I am but his fingers are small. It stands to reason that there must be a difference in the way in which we hold and use the bow. The difference between a great and a mediocre teacher lies in the fact that the first recognizes that bowing is an individual matter, different in the case of each individual pupil; and that the greatest perfection is attained by the development of the individual's capabilities within his own norm.

MARSICK AS A TEACHER

"Marsick was a teacher of this type. At each of the lessons I took from him at the *Conservatoire* (we went to him three days a week), he would give me a new *étude*—Gavinies, Rode, Fiorillo, Dont—to prepare for the next lesson. We also studied all of Paganini, and works by Ernst and Spohr. For our bow technique he employed difficult passages made into *études*. Scales—the violinist's daily bread—we practiced day in, day out. Marsick played the piano well, and could improvise marvelous accompaniments on his violin when his pupils played. I continued my studies with Marsick even after I left the *Conservatoire*. With him I believe that three essentials—absolute purity of pitch, equality of tone and sonority of tone, in connection with the bow—are the base on which everything else rests.

THE MECHANICAL VERSUS THE NATURAL IN VIOLIN PLAYING

"Sevčik's purely soulless and mechanical system has undoubtedly produced a number of excellent mechanicians of the violin.

But it has just as unquestionably killed real talent. Kubelik— there was a genuinely talented violinist! If he had had another teacher instead of Sevčik he would have been great, for he had great gifts. Even as it was he played well, but I consider him one of Sevčik's victims. As an illustration of how the technical point of view is thrust to the fore by this system I remember some fifteen years ago Kubelik and I were staying at the same villa in Monte-Carlo, where we were to play the Beethoven concerto, each of us, in concert, two days apart. Kubelik spent the livelong day before the concert practicing Sevčik exercises. I read and studied Beethoven's score, but did not touch my violin. I went to hear Kubelik play the concerto, and he played it well; but then, so did I, when my turn came. And I feel sure I got more out of it musically and spiritually, than I would have if instead of concentrating on its meaning, its musical message, I had prepared the concerto as a problem in violin mechanics whose key was contained in a number of dry technical exercises arbitrarily laid down.

"Technique, in the case of the more advanced violinist, should not have a place in the foreground of his consciousness. I heard Rubinstein play when a boy—what did his false notes amount to compared with his wonderful manner of disclosing the spirit of the things he played! Planté, the Parisian pianist, a kind of keyboard cyclone, once expressed the idea admirably to an English society lady. She had told him he was a greater pianist than Rubinstein, because the latter played so many wrong notes. 'Ah, Madame,' answered Planté, 'I would rather be able to play Rubinstein's wrong notes than all my own correct ones.' A violinist's natural manner of playing is the one he should cultivate; since it is individual, it really represents him. And a teacher or a colleague of greater fame does him no kindness if he encourages him to distrust his own powers by too good naturedly 'showing' him how to do this, that or the other. I mean, when the student can work out his problem himself at the expense of a little initiative.

"When I was younger I once had to play Bach's *G minor Fugue* at a concert in Brussels. I was living at Ysaye's home, and since I had never played the composition in public before, I began to worry about its interpretation. So I asked Ysaye (thinking he would simply show me), 'How ought I to play this fugue?' The Master reflected a moment and then dashed my hopes by answering: *'Tu m'embêtes!'* ('You bore me!') 'This fugue should be played well, that's all!' At first I was angry, but thinking it over, I realized that if he had shown me, I would have played it just as he did; while what he wanted me to do was to work out my own version, and depend on my own initiative—which I did, for I had no choice. It is by means of concentration on the higher, the interpretative phases of one's Art that the technical side takes its proper, secondary place. Technique does not exist for me in the sense of a certain quantity of mechanical work which I must do. I find it out of the question to do absolutely mechanical technical work of any length of time. In realizing the three essentials of good violin playing which I have already mentioned, Ysaye and Sarasate are my ideals.

SARASATE

"All really good violinists are good artists. Sarasate, whom I knew so intimately and remember so well, was a pupil of Alard (my father's teacher). He literally sang on the violin, like a nightingale. His purity of intonation was remarkable; and his technical facility was the most extraordinary that I have ever seen. He handled his bow with unbelievable skill. And when he played, the unassuming grace of his movements won the hearts of his audiences and increased the enthusiasm awakened by his tremendous talent.

"We other violinists, all of us, occasionally play a false note, for we are not infallible; we may flat a little or sharp a little. But never, as often as I have heard Sarasate play, did I ever hear him play a wrong note, one not in perfect pitch. His Spanish things he played like a god! And he had a wonderful gift of phrasing which gave a charm hard to define to whatever he played. And playing in quartet—the greatest solo violinist does not always shine in this *genre*—he was admirable. Though he played all the standard repertory, Bach, Beethoven, etc., I can never forget his exquisite rendering of modern works, especially of a little composition by Raff, called *La Fée d'Amour*. He was the first to play the violin concertos of Saint-Saëns, Lalo and Max Bruch. They were all written for him, and I doubt whether they would have been composed had not Sarasate been there to play them. Of course, in his own Spanish music he was unexcelled—a whole school of violin playing was born and died with him! He had a hobby for collecting canes. He had hundreds of them of all kinds, and every sovereign in Europe had contributed to his collection. I know Queen Christina of Spain gave him no less than twenty. He once gave me a couple of his canes, a great sign of favor with him. I have often played quartet with Sarasate, for he adored quartet playing, and these occasions are among my treasured memories.

STRADIVARIUS AND GUARNERIUS PLAYERS

"My violin? It is a Stradivarius—the same which once belonged to the celebrated Baillot. I think it is good for a violin to rest, so during the three months when I am not playing in concert, I send my Stradivarius away to the instrument maker's, and only take it out about a month before I begin to play again in public. What do I use in the meantime? Caressa, the best violin maker in Paris, made me an exact copy of my own Strad, exact in every little detail. It is so good that sometimes, when circumstances compelled me to, I have used it in concert, though it lacks the tone-quality of the original. This under-study violin I can use for practice, and when I go back to the original, as far as the handling of the instrument is concerned, I never know the difference.

"But I do not think that every one plays to the best advantage on a Strad. I'm a believer in the theory that there are natural Guarnerius players and natural Stradivarius players; that certain artists do their best with the one, and certain others with the other. And I also believe that any one who is 'equally' good in both, is great on neither. The reason I believe in Guarnerius players and Stradivarius players as distinct is this. Some years ago I had a sudden call to play in Ostende. It was a concert engagement which I had overlooked, and when it was recalled to me I was playing golf in Brittany. I at once hurried to Paris to get my violin from Caressa, with whom I had left it, but—his safe, in which it had been put, and to which he only had the combination, was locked. Caressa himself was in Milan. I telegraphed him but found that he could not get back in time before the concert to release my violin. So I telegraphed Ysaye at Namur, to ask if he could loan me a violin for the concert. 'Certainly,' he wired back. So I hurried to his home and, with his usual generosity, he insisted on my taking both his treasured Guarnerius and his 'Hercules' Strad (afterwards stolen from him in Russia), in order that I might have my choice. His brother-in-law and some friends accompanied me from Namur to Ostende—no great distance—to hear the concert. Well, I played the Guarnerius at rehearsal, and when it was over, every one said to me, 'Why, what is the matter with your fiddle? (It was the one Ysaye always used.) It has no tone at all.' At the concert I played the Strad and secured a big tone that filled the hall, as every one assured me. When I brought back the violins to Ysaye I mentioned the circumstance to him, and he was so surprised and interested that he took them from the cases and played a bit, first on one, then on the other, a number of times. And invariably when he played the Strad (which, by the way, he had not used for years) he, Ysaye—imagine it!—could develop only a small tone; and when he played the Guarnerius, he never failed to develop that great, sonorous tone we all know and love so well. Take Sarasate, when he lived, Elman, myself—we all have the habit of the Stradivarius: on the other hand Ysaye and Kreisler are Guarnerius players *par excellence!*

"Yes, I use a wire E string. Before I found out about them I had no end of trouble. In New Orleans I snapped seven gut strings at a single concert. Some say that you can tell the difference, when listening, between a gut and a wire E. I cannot, and I know a good many others who cannot. After my last New York recital I had tea with Ysaye, who had done me the honor of attending it. 'What strings do you use?' he asked me, *à propos* to nothing in particular. When I told him I used a wire E he confessed that he could not have told the difference. And, in fact, he has adopted the wire E just like Kreisler, Maud Powell and others, and has told me that he is charmed with it—for Ysaye has had a great deal of trouble with his strings. I shall continue to use them even after the war, when it will be possible to obtain good gut strings again.

THE IDEAL PROGRAM

"The whole question of programs and program-making is an intricate one. In my opinion the usual recital program, piano, song or violin, is too long. The public likes the recital by a single vocal or instrumental artist, and financially and for other practical reasons the artist, too, is better satisfied with them. But are they artistically altogether satisfactory? I should like to hear Paderewski and Ysaye, Bauer and Casals, Kreisler and Hofmann all playing at the same recital. What a variety, what a wealth of contrasting artistic enjoyment such a concert would afford. There is nothing that is so enjoyable for the true artist as *ensemble* playing with his peers. Solo playing seems quite unimportant beside it.

"I recall as the most perfect and beautiful of all my musical memories, a string quartet and quintet (with piano) session in Paris, in my own home, where we played four of the loveliest chamber music works ever written in the following combination: Beethoven's *Seventh Quartet* (Ysaye, Vln. I, myself, Vln. II, Kreisler, viola—he plays it remarkably well—and Casals, cello); the Schumann *Quartet* (Kreisler, Vln. I, Ysaye, Vln. II, myself, viola and Casals, cello); and the Mozart *G major Quartet* (myself, Vln. I, Kreisler, Vln. II, Ysaye, viola and Casals, cello). Then we telephoned to Pugno, who came over and joined us and, after an excellent dinner, we played the César Franck *Piano Quintet*. It was the most enjoyable musical day of my life. A concert manager offered us a fortune to play in this combination— just two concerts in every capital in Europe.

"We have not enough variety in our concert programs—not enough collaboration. The truth is our form of concert, which usually introduces only one instrument or one group of instruments, such as the string quartet, is too uniform in color. I can enjoy playing a recital program of virtuose violin pieces well enough; but I cannot help fearing that many find it too unicolored. Practical considerations do not do away with the truth of an artistic contention, though they may often prevent its realization. What I enjoy most, musically, is to play together with another good artist. That is why I have had such great artistic pleasure in the joint recitals I have given with Harold Bauer. We could play things that were really worth while for each of us— for the piano parts of the modern sonatas call for a virtuose technical and musical equipment, and I have had more satisfaction from this *ensemble* work than I would have had in playing a long list of solo pieces.

"The ideal violin program, to play in public, as I conceive it, is one that consists of absolute music, or should it contain virtuose pieces, then these should have some definite musical quality of soul, character, elegance or charm to recommend them. I think one of the best programs I have ever played in America is that which I gave with Harold Bauer at Æolian Hall, New York, during the season of 1917–1918:

Sonata in B flat	Mozart
BAUER-THIBAUD	
Scenes from Childhood	Schumann
H. BAUER	
Poème	E. Chausson
J. THIBAUD	
Sonata	César Franck
BAUER-THIBAUD	

Or perhaps this other, which Bauer and I played in Boston, during November, 1913:

Kreutzer Sonata	Beethoven
BAUER-THIBAUD	
Sarabanda ⎫	
Giga ⎬	J. S. Bach
Chaconne ⎭	
J. THIBAUD	
Kreisleriana	Schumann
H. BAUER	
Sonata	César Franck
BAUER-THIBAUD	

Either of these programs is artistic from the standpoint of the compositions represented. And even these programs are not too short—they take almost two hours to play; while for my ideal program an hour-and-a-half of beautiful music would suffice. You will notice that I believe in playing the big, fine things in music; in serving roasts rather than too many *hors d'oeuvres* and pastry.

"On a solo program, of course, one must make some concessions. When I play a violin concerto it seems fair enough to give the public three or four nice little things, but—always pieces which are truly musical, not such as are only 'ear-ticklers.' Kreisler—he has a great talent for transcription—has made charming arrangements. So has Tivadar Nachéz, of older things, and Arthur Hartmann. These one can play as well as shorter numbers by Vieuxtemps and Wieniawski that are delightful, such as the former's *Ballade et Polonaise*, though I know of musical purists who disapprove of it. I consider this *Polonaise* on a level with Chopin's. Or take, in the virtuoso field, Sarasate's *Gypsy Airs*—they are equal to any Liszt Rhapsody. I have only recently discovered that Ysaye—my life-long friend—has written some wonderful original compositions: a *Poème élégiaque*, a *Chant d'hiver*, an *Extase* and a ms. trio for two violins and alto that is marvelous. These pieces were an absolute find for me, with the exception of the lovely *Chant d'hiver*, which I have already played in Paris, Brussels, Amsterdam and Berlin, and expect to make a feature of my programs this winter. You see, Ysaye is so modest about his own compositions that he does not attempt to 'push' them, even with his friends, hence they are not nearly as well known as they should be.

"I never play operatic transcriptions and never will. The music of the opera, no matter how fine, appears to me to have its proper place on the stage—it seems out of place on the violin recital program. The artist cannot be too careful in the choice of his shorter program pieces. And he can profit by the example set by some of the foremost violinists of the day. Ysaye, that great apostle of the truly musical, is a shining example. It is sad to see certain young artists of genuine talent disregard the remarkable work of their great contemporary, and secure easily gained triumphs with compositions whose musical value is *nil*.

"Sometimes the wish to educate the public, to give it a high standard of appreciation, leads an artist astray. I heard a well-known German violinist play in Berlin five years ago, and what do you suppose he played? Beethoven's *Trios* transcribed for violin and piano! The last thing in the world to play! And there was, to my astonishment, no critical disapproval of what he did. I regard it as little less than a crime.

"But this whole question of programs and repertory is one without end. Which of the great concertos do I prefer? That is a difficult question to answer off-hand. But I can easily tell you which I like least. It is the Tchaikovsky *Violin Concerto*—I would not exchange the first ten measures of Vieuxtemps's *Fourth Concerto* for the whole of Tchaikovsky's, that is from the musical point of view. I have heard the Tchaikovsky played magnificently by Auer and by Elman; but I consider it the worst thing the composer has written."

GUSTAV SAENGER

THE EDITOR AS A FACTOR IN "VIOLIN MASTERY"

The courts of editorial appeal presided over by such men as Wm. Arms Fisher, Dr. Theodore Baker, Gustav Saenger and others, have a direct relation to the establishment and maintenance of standards of musical mastery in general and, in the case of Gustav Saenger, with "Violin Mastery" in particular. For this editor, composer and violinist is at home with every detail of the educational and artistic development of his instrument, and a considerable portion of the violin music published in the United States represents his final and authoritative revision.

"Has the work of the editor any influence on the development of 'Violin Mastery'?" was the first question put to Mr. Saenger when he found time to see the writer in his editorial rooms. "In a larger sense I think it has," was the reply. "Mastery of any kind comes as a result of striving for a definite goal. In the case of the violin student the road of progress is long, and if he is not to stray off into the numerous by-paths of error, it must be liberally provided with sign-posts. These sign-posts, in the way of clear and exact indications with regard to bowing, fingering, interpretation, it is the editor's duty to erect. The student himself must provide mechanical ability and emotional instinct, the teacher must develop and perfect them, and the editor must neglect nothing in the way of explanation, illustration and example which will help both teacher and pupil to obtain more intimate insight into the musical and technical values. Yes, I think the editor may claim to be a factor in the attainment of 'Violin Mastery.'

GUSTAV SAENGER

OLD WINE IN NEW BOTTLES

"The work of the responsible editor of modern violin music must have constructive value, it must suggest and stimulate. When Kreutzer, Gavinies and Rode first published their work, little stress was laid on editorial revision. You will find little in the way of fingering indicated in the old editions of Kreutzer. It was not till long after Kreutzer's death that his pupil, Massart, published an excellent little book, which he called *The Art of Studying R. Kreutzer's Études* and which I have translated. It contains no less than four hundred and twelve examples specially designed to aid the student to master the *Études* in the spirit of their composer. Yet these studies, as difficult today as they were when first written, are old wine that need no bush, though they have gained by being decanted into new bottles of editorial revision.

"They have such fundamental value, that they allow of infinite variety of treatment and editorial presentation. Every student who has reached a certain degree of technical proficiency takes them up. Yet when studying them for the first time, as a rule it is all he can do to master them in a purely superficial way. When he has passed beyond them, he can return to them with greater technical facility and, because of their infinite variety, find that they offer him any number of new study problems. As with Kreutzer—an essential to 'Violin Mastery'—so it is with Rode, Fiorillo, and Gavinies. Editorial care has prepared the studies in distinct editions, such as those of Hermann and Singer, specifically for the student, and that of Emil Kross, for the advanced player. These editions give the work of the teacher a more direct proportion of result. The difference between the two types is mainly in the fingering. In the case of the student editions a simple, practical fingering of positive educational value is given; and the student should be careful to use editions of this kind, meant for him. Kross provides many of the *études* with fingerings which only the virtuoso player is able to apply. Aside from technical considerations the absolute musical beauty of many of these studies is great, and they are well suited for solo performance. Rode's *Caprices*, for instance, are particularly suited for

such a purpose, and many of Paganini's famous *Caprices* have
found a lasting place in the concert repertory, with piano accompaniments by artists like Kreisler, Eddy Brown, Edward Behm
and Max Vogrich—the last-named composer's three beautiful
'Characteristic Pieces' after Paganini are worth any violinist's
attention.

AMERICAN EDITORIAL IDEALS

"In this country those intrusted with editorial responsibility as
regards violin music have upheld a truly American standard of
independent judgment. The time has long since passed when
foreign editions were accepted on their face value, particularly
older works. In a word, the conscientious American editor of
violin music reflects in his editions the actual state of progress
of the art of violin playing as established by the best teachers
and teaching methods, whether the works in question represent
a higher or lower standard of artistic merit.

"And this is no easy task. One must remember that the peculiar construction of the violin with regard to its technical possibilities makes the presentation of a violin piece difficult from an
editorial standpoint. A composition may be so written that a
beginner can play it in the first position; and the same number
may be played with beautiful effects in the higher positions by
an artist. This accounts for the fact that in many modern editions of solo music for violin, double fingerings, for student and
advanced players respectively, are indicated—an essentially
modern editorial development. Modern instructive works by
such masters as Sevčik, Eberhardt and others have made technical problems more clearly and concisely get-at-able than did
the older methods. Yet some of these older works are by no
means negligible, though of course, in all classic violin literature, from Tartini on, Kreutzer, Spohr, Paganini, Ernst, each
individual artist represents his own school, his own method to
the exclusion of any other. Spohr was one of the first to devote
editorial attention to his own method, one which, despite its
age, is a valuable work, though most students do not know how
to use it. It is really a method for the advanced player, since it
presupposes a good deal of preliminary technical knowledge,

and begins at once with the higher positions. It is rather a series of study pieces for the special development of certain difficult phases, musical and technical, of the violinist's art, than a method. I have translated and edited the American edition of this work, and the many explanatory notes with which Spohr has provided it—as in his own *9th*, and the Rode *Concerto* (included as representative of what violin concertos really should be), the measures being provided with group numbers for convenience in reference—are not obsolete. They are still valid, and any one who can appreciate the ideals of the *Gesangsscene*, its beautiful *cantilene* and pure serenity, may profit by them. I enjoyed editing this work because I myself had studied with Carl Richter, a Spohr pupil, who had all his master's traditions.

THE MASTER VIOLINIST AS AN EDITOR

"That the editorial revisions of a number of our greatest living violinists and teachers have passed through my editorial rooms, on their way to press, is a fact of which I am decidedly proud. Leopold Auer, for instance, is one of the most careful, exact and practical of editors, and the fact is worth dwelling on since sometimes the great artist or teacher quite naturally forgets that those for whom he is editing a composition have neither his knowledge nor resources. Auer never loses sight of the composer's *own ideas*.

"And when I mention great violinists with whom I have been associated as an editor, Mischa Elman must not be forgotten. I found it at first a difficult matter to induce an artist like Elman, for whom no technical difficulties exist, to seriously consider the limitations of the average player in his fingerings and interpretative demands. Elman, like every great virtuoso of his caliber, is influenced in his revisions by the manner in which he himself does things. I remember in one instance I could see no reason why he should mark the third finger for a *cantilena* passage where a certain effect was desired, and questioned it. Catching up his violin he played the note preceding it with his second finger, then instead of slipping the second finger down the string, he took the next note with the third, in such a way that a most exquisite *legato* effect, like a breath, the echo of a sigh, was secured. And the beauty of tone color in this instance not only proved his point, but has led me invariably to examine very closely a fingering on the part of a master violinist which represents a departure from the conventional—it is often the technical key to some new beauty of interpretation or expression.

"Fritz Kreisler's individuality is also reflected in his markings and fingerings. Of course those in his 'educational' editions are strictly meant for study needs. But in general they are difficult and based on his own manner and style of playing. As he himself has remarked: 'I could play the violin just as well with three as with four fingers.' Kreisler is fond of 'fingered' octaves, and these, because of his abnormal hand, he plays with the first and third fingers, where virtuose players, as a rule, are only too happy if they can play them with the first and fourth. To verify this individual character of his revisions, one need only glance at his edition of Godowsky's '12 Impressions' for violin—in every case the fingerings indicated are difficult in the extreme; yet they supply the key to definite effects, and since this music is intended for the advanced player, are quite in order.

"The ms. and revisions of many other distinguished artists have passed through my hands. Theodore Spiering has been responsible for the educational detail of classic and modern works; Arthur Hartmann—a composer of marked originality—Albert Spalding, Eddy Brown, Francis MacMillan, Max Pilzer, David Hochstein, Richard Czerwonky, Cecil Burleigh, Edwin Grasse, Edmund Severn, Franz C. Bornschein, Leo Ornstein, Rubin Goldmark, Louis Pershinger, Louis Victor Saar—whose ms. always look as though engraved—have all given me opportunities of seeing the best the American violin composer is creating at the present time.

EDITORIAL DIFFICULTIES

"The revisional work of the master violinist is of very great importance, but often great artists and distinguished teachers hold radically different views with regard to practically every detail of their art. And it is by no means easy for an editor like myself, who is finally responsible for their editions, to harmonize a hundred conflicting views and opinions. The fiddlers best qualified to speak with authority will often disagree absolutely regarding the use of a string, position, up-bow or down-bow. And besides meeting the needs of student and teacher, an editor-in-chief must bear in mind the artistic requirements of the music itself. In many cases the divergence in teaching standards reflects the personal preferences for the editions used. Less ambitious teachers choose methods which make the study of the violin as *easy* as possible for *them*; rather than those which—in the long run—may be most advantageous for the *pupil*. The best editions of studies are often cast aside for trivial reasons, such as are embodied in the poor excuse that 'the fourth finger is too frequently indicated.' According to the old-time formulas, it was generally accepted that ascending passages should be played on the open strings and descending ones using the fourth finger. It stands to reason that the use of the fourth finger involves more effort, is a greater tax of strength, and that the open string is an easier playing proposition. Yet a really perfected technique demands that the fourth finger be every bit as strong and flexible as any of the others. By nature it is shorter and weaker, and beginners usually have great trouble with it— which makes perfect control of it all the more essential! And yet teachers, contrary to all sound principle and merely to save effort—temporarily—for themselves and their pupils, will often reject an edition of a method or book of studies merely because in its editing the fourth finger has not been deprived of its proper chance of development. I know of cases where, were it not for the guidance supplied by editorial revision, the average teacher would have had no idea of the purpose of the studies he was using. One great feature of good modern editions of classical study works, from Kreutzer to Paganini, is the double editorial numeration: one giving the sequence as in the original editions; the other numbering the studies in order of technical difficulty, so that they may be practiced progressively.

A UNIQUE COLLECTION OF VIOLIN STUDIES

"What special editorial work of mine has given me the greatest personal satisfaction in the doing? That is a hard question to answer. Off-hand I might say that, perhaps, the collection of progressive orchestral studies for advanced violinists which I have compiled and annotated for the benefit of the symphony orchestra player is something that has meant much to me personally. Years ago, when I played professionally—long before the days of 'miniature' orchestra scores—it was almost impossible for an ambitious young violinist to acquaint himself with the first and second violin parts of the great symphonic works. Prices of scores were prohibitive—and though in such works as the Brahms symphonies, for instance, the 'concertmaster's' part should be studied from score, in its relation to the rest of the *partitura*—often, merely to obtain a first violin part, I had to acquire the entire set of strings. So when I became an editor I determined, in view of my own unhappy experiences and that of many others, to give the aspiring fiddler who really wanted to 'get at' the violin parts of the best symphonic music, from Bach to Brahms and Richard Strauss, a chance to do so. And I believe I solved the problem in the five books of the *Modern Concert-Master,* which includes all those really difficult and important passages in the great repertory works of the symphony orchestra that offer violinistic problems. My only regret is that the grasping attitude of European publishers prevented the representation of certain important symphonic numbers. Yet, as it stands, I think I may say that the five encyclopedic books of the collection give the symphony concertmaster every practical opportunity to gain orchestral routine, and orchestral mastery.

A NEW CLASSIFICATION OF VIOLIN LITERATURE

"What I am inclined to consider, however, as even more important, in a sense, than my editorial labors is a new educational classification of violin literature, one which practically covers the entire field of violin music, and upon which I have been engaged for several years. Insomuch as an editor's work helps in the acquisition of 'Violin Mastery,' I am tempted to think this catalogue will be a contribution of real value.

"As far as I know there does not at present exist any guide or hand-book of violin literature in which the fundamental question of grading has been presented *au fond*. This is not strange, since the task of compiling a really valid and logically graded guide-book of violin literature is one that offers great difficulties from almost every point of view.

"Yet I have found the work engrossing, because the need of a book of the kind which makes it easy for the teacher to bring his pupils ahead more rapidly and intelligently by giving him an oversight of the entire teaching-material of the violin and under clear, practical heads in detail order of progression is making itself more urgently felt every day. In classification (there are seven grades and a preparatory grade), I have not chosen an easier and conventional plan of *general* consideration of difficulties; but have followed a more systematic scheme, one more closely related to the study of the instrument itself. Thus, my *Preparatory Grade* contains only material which could be advantageously used with children and beginners, those still struggling with the simplest elementary problems—correct drawing of the bow across the open strings, in a certain rhythmic order, and the first use of the fingers. And throughout the grades are special sub-sections for special difficulties, special technical and other problems. In short, I cannot help but feel that I have compiled a real guide, one with a definite educational value, and not a catalogue, masquerading as a violinistic Baedeker.

VIOLIN EDITIONS "MADE IN AMERICA"

"One of the most significant features of the violin guide I have mentioned is, perhaps, the fact that its contents largely cover the whole range of violin literature in American editions. There was a time, years ago, when 'made in Germany' was accepted as a certificate of editorial excellence and mechanical perfection. Those days have long since passed, and the American edition has come into its own. It has reached a point of development where it is of far more practical and musically stimulating value than any European edition. For American editions of violin music do not take so much for granted! They reflect in the highest degree the needs of students and players in smaller places throughout the country, and where teachers are rare or nonexistent they do much to supply instruction by meticulous regard for all detail of fingering, bowing, phrasing, expression, by insisting in explanatory annotation on the correct presentation of authoritative teaching ideas and principles. In a broader sense 'Violin Mastery' knows no nationality; but yet we associate the famous artists of the day with individual and distinctively national trends of development and 'schools.' In this connection I am convinced that one result of this great war of world liberation we have waged, one by-product of the triumph of the democratic truth, will be a notably 'American' ideal of 'Violin Mastery,' in the musical as well as the technical sense. And in the development of this ideal I do not think it is too much to claim that American editions of violin music, and those who are responsible for them, will have done their part."